Descent:

A Heroine's Journey Into The Shadowlands Of "Bipolar Disorder"

Evelyn Scogin

chipmunkapublishing
the mental health publisher

Published by
Chipmunkapublishing
PO Box 6872
Brentwood
Essex CM13 1ZT
United Kingdom

http://www.chipmunkapublishing.com

Edited by Faith Mmadubuike

ISBN   978-1-84991-861-9

Chipmunkapublishing gratefully acknowledge the support of Arts Council England.

Unless someone like you cares a whole awful lot,
nothing is going to get better. It's not.

Unless...

Dr. Seuss

Theodore Geisel

To all who have found

their voices of dissent

now and in the future.

Descent

Acknowledgments

To my family chosen and otherwise who have been supportive of me even when they don't necessarily agree with my opinions on this subject. I love you all the more for your support through adversity.

My thanks go especially to my sister Katherine who gave me a home and emotional support when I needed it most. Through your generous and gregarious spirit we met the person who was to make the biggest difference in both our lives. You remind me daily what it means to be a totally giving person especially when it is not convenient.

During the course of this passage of my life I met several individuals and groups of people who taught me what it is to devote yourself to a cause you believe in. I give thanks to Jim Moore, Lee Spillar and all the folks at CCHR. Your actions improve life daily for all. You guys rock.

Lastly I cannot express enough gratitude to Dr. John Breeding who my sister met by chance but who changed my life in ways I am still learning. You taught me many things not the least of which is that I have the right to say no and make my own decisions. You gave me a voice again which I now use in dissent. I will never forget all you have taught me. Many Thanks.

Descent

Table of Contents

Descent

FOREWORD

I am delighted to introduce this powerful memoir of one woman's near destruction and re-emergence from psychiatric assault. When I first met Evelyn Scogin in 2006 she had been severely hurt and debilitated by those in the psychiatric system to whom she had reached out for help. She was very overweight and could barely walk. Her consciousness was dulled and her ability to communicate was limited. She had a variety of severe health problems, and she was on full-time psychiatric disability.

Evelyn's memory and cognitive abilities were severely impaired by the intense, brain-disabling psychopharmaceutical cocktail she was taking, and the residual effects of the 31 brain-damaging electroshock assaults she had suffered over a 6-month period. It is a tragedy and a shame that Evelyn, like countless others, experienced so much unnecessary suffering at the hands of so-called mental health professionals. Nevertheless, she showed up, with her sister Kathy's support; an inkling of her dormant spirit remained. Over the ensuing years, it has been my privilege and honor to witness the hard-earned recovery and transformation of Evelyn Scogin.

Counseling on hurts and distress is hard work, but not so complicated really. There is a lot of listening, and support and encouragement for emotional expression and the release of trauma. However, as a psychologist practicing today, it is very troubling to see so many layers of hurt and disability piled onto original traumas by my own mental health profession. Evelyn's life is a horrific example of iatrogenic trauma caused by psychiatric treatment. I wish I could say it was an anomaly, but in fact it is business as usual in psychiatry. I witnessed Evelyn's disillusionment and shattering of naïve trust in the "helpers" who had hurt and betrayed her, the working through of overwhelming fear and grief, the determined and courageous withdrawal from so many psychiatric drugs, and the painstaking remediation of the brain damage caused by those drugs and the electroshock. It has been especially inspiring to see Evelyn reclaim her power and her voice. When she is quoted in the *Washington Post*, and when she is bending the ear of politicians on mental health policy, I am in awe.

Evelyn Scogin is one of the most courageous and determined women I have ever met. Her story represents many psychiatric survivors who have beaten the odds and freed themselves from the tyranny of oppression by labeling, drugs and electroshock. Evelyn has become a clear, intelligent, persistent and passionate voice for liberation from psychiatric oppression. This clear and truthful memoir is a wonderful plain speech antidote to psychiatric jargon and obfuscation. It is also a guidebook that will help others to find their way in the face of great challenges, and false and dangerous ways of psychiatric "treatment." Finally, Evelyn's story is an inspiring model of the heroic resilience of the human spirit.

Dr. John Breeding

Introduction

When John suggested to me that I write my story and publish it I had no idea where to start or where the story would end. The story took about 8 years to unfold with the last half consisting of therapy and the writing of this episode in my life. The first year of writing was in fits and starts however, I found that with each passage I wrote I was able to work through the fears and emotions that went with them. In turn as I was able to work through the feelings surrounding an event this allowed space for me to face the next memory.

Another piece that surfaced as I worked was my ability to find my voice and advocate for myself and others in very powerful ways. None of this growth would have happened if not for the support of many family and friends along the ways.

My story began with my descent down a very slippery slope that unfortunately many people are now finding themselves on. The idea presented by mainstream psychiatry that emotional discharge is bad for us and should be avoided at all costs is at the bottom of that slope and for me a very deep pit was at the bottom of the hill. The pit was called being labeled mentally ill and being given drugs and electroshock until I did not know who or where I was.

Through a chain of events my older sister found the group of individuals who were able to show me not only the pit I was in but they gave me the ladder I could use to climb to freedom. The group was the Citizens Coalition for Human Rights and John Breeding the man who helped me climb out of the pit one rung at a time.

With his caring counseling I was able to see that I was not stuck in the biopsychiatry pit forever.

There were times that I slipped down several rungs, but John was always there to support me until I could continue climbing again. I have finally climbed out of that pit. By writing and speaking about my story I have filled in that pit forever. I have changed in many ways but in the end that is what spiritual growth is about. Many people who knew me before do not agree with my point of view, but that will not stop the telling of it. I only hope that the people who need to find their way out of their own pit will find my story enlightening and will in the end be able to share their story of descent and recovery.

Evelyn Scogin

2012

Losing My Mind and
The Great Unknown

It is such a subtle thing
Especially in the beginning
Losing ones' mind
I hardly seemed to notice.

My behavior began to change
My emotions began to change
My employer was concerned
My friends and family were very concerned

As my mind was slipping
I hardly seemed to notice.
I went to my family doctor
He told me I was depressed and prescribed paxil
I began to feel worse…

The paxil made me suicidal
My mind slipped another notch
I tried to kill myself
(so they say?)
I hardly seemed to notice.

I was in and out of a mental hospital
I was "disabled" and unable to work
I could no longer pursue my calling
My sisters had to take care of me.
And yet I hardly seemed to notice.

My mind had gone away from me
I don't know where it went
Into the "Great Unknown"
On the dark side of the moon?

Descent

Chapter One

The Beginning

After being subjected to a degradation ceremony known as psychiatric examination, [the patient] is bereft of his civil liberties in being imprisoned in a totalitarian institution known as a "mental" hospital. More completely, more radically than anywhere else in our society, he is invalidated as a human being.

R. D. Laing (1927-1989), British psychiatrist, *The Politics of Experience*, 5, 1967(1)

The problem with telling a story such as mine is not the story, but where to begin the telling of it. I can't tell you the exact beginning as it probably started when I was a child. However, the greatest portion of the story began in 2003. That is a guess of course because as with many people who have suffered through biopsychiatry much of my memory is confused or lost.

In the beginning I was a 47 year old Special Education Teacher. I had been teaching in the classroom for about 6 years. I came to teaching after working for about 15 years prior to that with multi-handicapped individuals of all ages. This to me was not just a job but a calling, a calling I kind of fell into after a life changing event. I had just gone through a divorce. Although it was not particularly adversarial it definitely changed my life. The other major factor acting on my life was chronic wide spread pain and headaches. I had been to doctor after doctor for most of my adult life and they could not tell me what was causing my pain.

Like many other people, I believed that doctors know everything and can do no wrong. I also believed that if something is wrong with you it must have a biological base and therefore a cure or at least an effective treatment. Of course, I now know that to be a false belief, but found that out a little too late to prevent my involving myself in bio- psychiatry. Being at my wits end and having no other recourse I sought help from my family doctor. Sometime in late 2003 I told him I was having continuing pain and no one seemed to know what was wrong with me. He told me I was depressed, who wouldn't be with all the pain and pressure at work and home, and he prescribed paxil. I being the obedient little patient took the prescription and filled it and began taking the medication. All of this without even a referral for therapy of any kind. I took that medicine every day just as prescribed until I literally stopped thinking.

That is the hideous, insidious nature of those drugs; they are designed to keep you from thinking about anything especially what is really bothering you. Like most Americans I accepted that the doctor would not prescribe something that was bad for me after all he was the doctor. He had diagnosed me with an illness and therefore this pill must be the cure or at least treatment that would alleviate all of my symptoms. This of course is not true because I had and have no illness. Yes I am and was emotionally upset and needed help, someone to talk to about what I was going through. Of course, this is the exact opposite of what happened. I went on this way for some time and then in the spring of 2004 the pain in my right foot became unbearable on top of all of my other pain. So what did I do? I did what any self-respecting American citizen would do I went back to the same doctor and he sent me to a podiatrist.

Of course this doctor listened to me for maybe about five seconds, took an x-ray and diagnosed me with heel spurs. The doctor gave me shots of cortisone in my foot and told me I needed surgery. The only recourse was surgery; there was no other help for my pain. As usual I afterward learned that a lot of podiatrists now treat this condition with physical therapy as the surgery is usually ineffective. Well I followed the doctor's instructions just like any good patient and scheduled the surgery for the summer when I was already off work (the three best things about teaching being June, July, and August). The doctor explained that they would use a laser and partially cut through the tendon in the arch of my foot. This would relax the foot back into proper alignment and thus relieve my pain. He further explained this would put me off my foot for about two weeks and I should be completely recovered in about a month. Note to self: in future ask the doctor what his idea of completely recovered is. Needless to say it took me longer than that to recover. I can't at this moment tell you when that was because it was long after I had completely lost what was left of myself.

That same fall I returned to work and tried to continue as usual. However, I was unable to do so because so many things were going on at once, and I became overwhelmed. Family situations were deteriorating. My pain was worse than ever. The stress at work was getting to me and my performance was suffering because of all of these things and probably many more I don't even recall. In my family we learned at a young age to not talk about what was really bothering us. This is probably not that unusual an occurrence but was a big part of what came after. You see at that same young age I also learned that if I wanted to have the love and respect of people around me I must be the "good girl". Thus I literally would rather die than have someone I loved and or respected be disappointed in me. So when things started to unravel I thought it was all my fault. If only I had done a better job or been a better daughter or sister, things would be okay. If someone else had come to me and said that I would have sincerely told them that was not true and they were not at fault for everything that goes wrong in life. However, it would never have occurred to me that I was doing that exact same thing to myself. All things being equal if I had been able to talk to someone about what was bothering me at the time I might have seen what I was doing to myself. Standing on the other side of this episode today, I know I would still need to have gone through the emotional upheaval I went through in order to resolve my upset. The thing that might have changed was how I was able to work through the dark tunnel to the other side.

As I mentioned before I returned to work as usual that fall. I loved working with my students; my work and my family are really what I lived for. Also during this time my father, who had been living with my older sister decided, he could no longer live with her and decided to move to Austin, Texas to be near my younger sister and I. My father was definitely not the easiest person to get along with. In fact, although I loved him dearly, I can say he had a big piece in the emotional upheaval I was experiencing. My father was one of the most bigoted people I have ever known. I can say for sure that he had a great part in shaping the person I was to later become. At the time he moved to Austin he was in his eighties and was having more and more difficulty living and caring for himself. He, however, insisted that he move out of the house with my older sister as she was, in his view robbing him blind, and move to Austin to be near my younger sister and me. We did not have room for him in our house so we found an apartment nearby that he could live in. Having been pulled out of school by third grade to help on the family farm my father was illiterate (until my Mother helped him learn to read), and he was unable to even keep his own checkbook. My father grew up in a time that men did men's work and women stayed home and took care of the house, kids and him. This is what my Mother did for most of her life. Then when my mother died at the age of 59 from metastatic breast cancer my father did not know what to do. He could not take care of himself or his bills or anything. About 3 months later he moved in with a woman he had known for many years through the Moose Lodge him and my mother both attended. She had been widowed several years before and was alone; they connected again through their lodge and then moved in together. She was able to help my father take care of himself for several years. After she died my older sister and her two sons moved in with my father until he moved to Austin when my younger sister and I took over his care. The care of my father was definitely a large stressor in my life at that time. My younger sister and I also had a very good friend from our work that helped out with the care of my father.

My younger sister would take care of my father's meds and his bills (she always being better with finances) and I would clean house (with the help of our friend). My sister and I would also do his shopping and sometimes prepare his meals and we all took turns taking him to his doctor's appointments. This is where my memory starts to get really fuzzy. My father evidently became increasingly ill and unable to care for himself. My older sister who later moved to Austin (I found out later that this was at the behest of my younger sister), and lived in the apartment complex next to my father's. I do not remember most of these events. This is one of my greatest frustrations and a source of great grief for me. My father one day fell out of bed and then got sick and was in the hospital with an intestinal infection which can be deadly. Evidently the first time this happened he got better in a few days and went back to his apartment. Everything kind of continued on from there.

One somewhat clear memory from that period of time was Christmas of 2004 when we brought my father to me and my younger sister's house for the holiday. We had not gotten to spend the holiday together as a family for a couple of years, I think. Again this is just an impression as my time line is somewhat skewed. I remember clearly bringing him into the house in his motorized wheelchair. He spent Christmas Eve night with us; although I don't remember that night, I do remember parts of that day. We had breakfast together with my whole family (this is the last time I remember my entire family being together for the holiday). When I was a child the entire holiday season was of great import to me. I remember spending every holiday together even as an adult until that time. Many things have happened since that have put barriers up between various family and friends and that time of year is much different for me now.

For me when there is upheaval in my life I tend to cling to those ritualized things that gave my life great meaning. I feel sure this is true for most people. However, as you might guess I lost most of those things and people, and life made no sense for me anymore. The terrible thing about all of this chaos is that you don't realize what is happening to you until it is too late. I became more confused and despondent as days became weeks until I was just going through the motions of my daily life and nothing made sense anymore. As I said I had gone to a doctor and he had prescribed paxil which I took faithfully. I had no idea that the drug paxil, was causing a large portion of my confusion and no one suggested the one thing that would have helped me. No one, especially the doctor, suggested that I go to a counselor. I just assumed that he would suggest that if I needed it. I was still thinking like, a good little patient that the doctor knew best. So I soldiered on not knowing that I was fast sliding downhill into a quicksand I knew no way out of. In September of that year (2004), I did the one thing that was sure to bring down the wrath of biopsychiatry on my head.

Before continuing, I should insert my definition of biopsychiatry. This is the current thought in psychiatry that all emotional upsets can be classified biologically as they define all emotional upheaval as biologically based. Most people today assume this to be true as did I until I did a little research on my own. The psychiatric community that is in control at the moment further supposes if all upsets are biologically based then they should be treated with pills,(the backup treatment being electroshock),and not caring and common sense. The biopsychiatric system works with the pharmaceutical companies to drug us all into oblivion.

The thing that I did to bring about my final downfall happened in late September. I was feeling bad one night and as I have been trained to do I turned to my medicine cabinet. I was having pain and I went to get a couple of antihistamines. I don't remember a lot clearly from this point forward but this one memory was burnt into my brain. I don't remember if it was day or night but I went to get my medicine and poured out a couple of pills in my hand. I remember staring at the pills for a long time. Then I stared for an equally long period of time at the pills remaining in the bottle. As I stood there looking from the bottle to the pills in my hand my one clear thought was if I take a couple and feel better then if I take all of them I will feel even better and so I did. I then went to bed. I don't know how much time elapsed but I eventually got up and went into the hallway as I heard my older sister come in. I remembered it being my younger sister whom I lived with but later found out it was my older sister. I looked at her and said I think I did something stupid. I proceeded to tell her I had taken the whole bottle of pills. At this point I know I did not feel scared or confused or feeling much of anything. In fact she could have probably told me it was a good idea to go jump in the lake and I would have done it feeling nothing about it. I tell a lot of the remaining story kind of like a third person as that is exactly how it felt.

When I was a child I had a similar experience after an accident. I was 13 and it was Friday 31 October, this day was one of my favorite times of the year. I was at the time a monkey and climbed everything I could reach. In my middle school playground there was a retaining wall. On one side it was ten foot high and had all kinds of pipes sticking out of it and on the other it was only two or three feet high and the top was about 18 inches across. This was irresistible to my friends and I. Every day before school and at lunch break we would scale the wall using the pipes then pretend we were walking a tightrope to cross the top then climb back down the short side and proceed to do this over and over again as kids are wont to do. This particular morning it was chilly and we were involved in our favorite pastime. I was walking across the top and came to a point on the wall where you had to grab the end of the fence that joined the wall at this point and then move past the fence and continue to the end of the wall. As I grabbed for the fence I found only air. Suddenly as my body hurled through space to the asphalt below I was watching myself fall to the ground. I remember feeling the air leave my body as I hit the ground but feeling nothing else. Now as this was many (I shuddered to think how many) years ago the teacher thought nothing of standing me up and rushing me to the nurses' office. From this point until I arrived late to my first class I remember hearing everyone and everything around me but nothing did I remember seeing. These well-meaning teachers took me to the nurse, me limping the whole way. I landed on my left hip and unbeknownst to me or anyone else I fractured my hip; this I later found out in my adulthood. The nurse evidently talked to me and I must have sounded coherent and must have appeared fine as they sent me on to class. Now in my middle school the nurse was on the upper floor of one building and my class was in the top floor of the other building. I do not remember seeing anything until my foot stepped onto the top floor of the building which housed my class. This is the same detachment I felt from myself at the time I took those pills. This detachment was almost euphoric as I sensed neither pain nor emotion; it was as if all of this was happening to another person. This same detachment alternated with great periods of emotional upheaval for the next three or four years. If you have ever undergone great emotional distress even for a short period of time you can understand why this detachment becomes important. It was one of my body's ways of protecting myself. When I was 13 it protected me from feeling the pain in my leg and as an adult it protected my mind from confronting the issues I was avoiding at all costs.

When I told my older sister that I had taken a bottle of antihistamine, the nurse in her kicked in and she rushed me to the hospital. The thing I remember most from that trip to the emergency room is that I had to drink this huge container of activated charcoal. I sat for many hours while I drank this thick gray sludge that was very sweet. While I was there I talked to the nurse and the doctor as well as my sister but none of that is attached to memories of this event. At some point I agreed to go to one of the local privately run mental hospital Shoal Creek. It probably did not take much encouragement to get me to go to the hospital as I did not know what I was doing. So anything the people in charge told me to do I did. I am sure they felt it was the best thing for me; after all, I had tried to "commit suicide". I was so numb at that point I can't honestly say if that was true or not. Even my older sister thought this was the best thing for me to do and encouraged me to go.

"Maximum Benefit Achieved"

Maximum benefit achieved.
What is that?
I was upset and crying
No benefit achieved

I followed their rules
I went to their classes
Still I was not allowed
off the floor.
No benefit here

Finally I took all their drugs
I took their electroshock therapy
I stopped crying and talking
I felt sadder and more confused than ever
No longer working
I sat alone all day
working puzzles and watching television

The psychiatrist released me from the hospital
"Maximum Benefit Achieved"

Descent

Chapter 2

Descent

"The multitude of men and women choose the less adventurous way of the comparatively unconscious civic and tribal routines. But these seekers, too, are saved— by virtue of the inherited symbolic aids of society, the rites of passage, the grace-yielding sacraments, given to mankind of old by the redeemers and handed down through millenniums. It is only those who know neither an inner call nor an outer doctrine whose plight truly is desperate; that is to say, most of us today, in this labyrinth without and within the heart. Alas, where is the guide, that fond virgin, Ariadne, to supply the simple clue that will give us courage to face the Minotaur, and the means then to find our way to freedom when the monster has been met and slain?"
— *Joseph Campbell*, *The Hero With a Thousand Faces(1)*

I was taken by ambulance to Shoal Creek where they proceeded to sign me in. Having never had any contact with the psychiatric community I had no idea what to expect. I was still disconnected from myself so I just did what the personnel at the psychiatric hospital told me to. First you have to fill out all of this paperwork with all kinds of personal information. I must have had help from my sister as there is no way I could remember all of this information. Then I had a battery of psychological tests that I was taken through. I don't know how I even answered as I was doing good to tell anyone my name. I don't think I had slept for several days and here they are trying to administer a test with accurate results. If this had been a student of mine and I was told to administer a test with my student in such a state I would have refused. There is no way to get accurate results when the person being tested is in that confused a state, not to mention all of those tests are subjective. After all of this then I talked to the on call psychiatric intern for maybe 5 minutes and then he wrote orders for my admission. As if all of this is not overwhelming enough I was presented with all of these different legal papers to sign. This is called "informed consent". I know I was shown papers and I know I signed them, but I could not have told you what I signed if my life depended on it, and I guess it did. One thing they never told me was that the minute I signed those papers I was no longer a voluntary patient. I would have to stay for at least 72 hours before I could leave. Of course I was unaware I had any choice in anything during this whole time period.

This next part is only just now clear in my mind as I write it. In fact I had to stop writing at this point and my therapist helped me step through this whole experience so that I could write about it as it was very traumatic to me. I was taken to the floor I was assigned to and greeted by two techs on the floor. These women took me to a small room that I was to find out later was used also by the psychiatrist to talk to their patients. The room was nothing but a small gray square with all the cinder block walls painted gray. The only furniture in the room was two brown folding chairs. The women asked me to remove all of my clothes for them to search. During this time I was never given a sheet or gown to cover myself. I had to sit naked on a cold brown metal folding chair while they checked my clothes for anything I could hurt myself with. Then they asked me to stand, still naked, while one of them searched my body for any injuries or bruises. When they found an injury the other woman would take pictures of them with a Polaroid camera. Afterward they returned my clothes to me and waited while I dressed myself. All of this time the two women were talking to each other about, well I don't remember what, as if I were not even there, as if I were not even important, I was just a chore, a part of the woodwork. Oh wait there was no woodwork.

Now it was about 4 or 5 in the morning so they did not bother to explain anything else to me, not that I would have understood it, but instead escorted me to my room and explained where everything was and left me alone. This first night I did not have a roommate. I put on my pajamas and crawled into bed. I remember laying there in the dark not really understanding what had just happened to me curled up holding a pillow and feeling like I was a child again afraid of the dark and needing my mother only she was not there; no one was there; in fact I was barely there. If you have ever stayed in any type of hospital you know how much rest you actually get even though that is what you really need. At about 6am that morning the hospital started to rouse. At seven one of the technicians came in and told me my doctor was there to talk to me. I was still in my pajamas but was escorted back to the same room in which I was searched the night before. At this point I was greeted by my psychiatrist, Dr. Lam. I had never met a psychiatrist in my life and I wrongly assumed he was there to help me work out what emotional problems I had. That could not have been further from the truth. He stood and greeted me and was very serious and polite. I sat shivering on the cold hard surface of the folding chair across from him and waited for him to tell me what to do.

At this point I had no idea I had any choice in anything. I was raised that you do not go against any authority, but most especially a "doctor". So while I waited he read through all of the paperwork from the night before. I had no idea what any of it said or meant and still do not know what was decided about me by any of the people I had talked to, but as it turns out these opinions of people I had met and talked to for only a few minutes each was treated as absolute fact. Nothing I said or did after changed their minds about who or what I was. In fact what I said and did only made things worse. If I disagreed with anything they said I was from that time forward a personality disorder. Of course I knew nothing of any of these opinions until after all of these things occurred when friends were able to help me get at least some of my records. As I say I sat there while Dr. Lam ignored me in favor of the paperwork he was so focused on. He talked to me for about five minutes, though I could not tell you what he said. What I can tell you is that I was the good little patient and just went along with what he told me. I was of course immediately put on several psychotropic drugs which was really the extent of what Dr. Lam did for me. When he was finished prescribing he stood, shook my hand and left. I returned to my room not understanding anything that was going on around me.

A few minutes later a tech came down the hall hollering that it was time to line up to get meds and line up to go down for breakfast. I hurriedly dressed and went to the reception area in front of the elevators. Across from the elevators was the nurse's station where we lined up for our medications. Before I was given my pills I was given a paper to sign for each new medication given for the first time. Each paper listed what the medication was and what it was for and I was asked to sign. I was told that if I wanted they would print out information about the side effects and interactions for each. I of course said that was okay as I believed Dr. Lam would never prescribe anything that would or could hurt me. I then swallowed what they handed me without further thought. If there is one piece of advice I would give anyone it would be to <u>never</u> just accept that what the doctor prescribes. Today I always question my doctors about what their treatment is and why. Second I always do my own research about treatment options this goes for something as simple as high blood pressure to something as serious as cancer. You should always know what is being given to you and what reactions it can and will cause in your body. Then you should decide if you want to accept the risks of that procedure. Remember you always have the right to say "No" in a loud and clear voice. I was programmed to accept the doctor's word as fact. This happens all of the time in the medical industry but most especially in bio-psychiatry. This reaction is also more prevalent with women and older adults. I know that this makes life easier for the doctors but ultimately made my life hell. After all of these events it took me a couple of years and some incredible amount of searching to find a group of doctors that I could work with. For me that means a doctor that will talk to me and be patient with me while I do my own research about drugs and procedures and allow me to say no. Some doctors will not continue to work with you if you say no and I had to learn to stand my ground when it comes to my body. To do this I have to be ready to put up with a longer wait time in the office as the doctor in question takes longer with each of her patients. To me my health is worth the wait.

After taking my pills I joined the group waiting by the elevator to go down for breakfast. I was shocked to find that the doors were locked and we had to be escorted anywhere we went. I thought I was a voluntary patient and could sign myself out anytime I wanted. It seems that when you sign yourself in after a suicide attempt that you are no longer a voluntary patient, a fact that they never tell you. So now I was locked on this floor with people I did not know and I had to be escorted everywhere. The tech informed me the doctor ordered that I was not allowed to leave the floor for meals or outside time. I had no idea the doctor ordered this or why. Since I don't go down for meals I get to eat what they bring to me even if I don't like it. The people who are not allowed off the floor receive their meals in the day room. I wandered in looking around trying to decide what I should do. Another patient told me where to find my meal. Since at the time I was eating totally vegetarian I only ate my cereal and drank my juice. I then went into a corner and sat on a sofa by myself not knowing what else to do. I don't remember feeling particularly afraid of anyone there; I just felt so lost that I pulled away from everything and curled into myself. I just sat there on that stupid plastic sofa and stared into space while the world went on around me. I had unconsciously decided that the safest thing for me to do was to divorce myself from the environment in which I found myself.

Later that morning, after breakfast, one of the nurse technicians came into the day room a large living room area with chairs, sofas, tables, TV and VCR used for free time. She laid out the rules and explained the morning routine. She also told us the schedule was posted on the white board in the front hall near the elevators and phones. I don't remember most of the rules except that during group times we could not use the TV or day room and the phones are turned off except during lunch and after all groups were finished. You could only make local phone calls and only be on the phone for 5 minutes at a time. Your family or friends could only call if they had your personal ID number and you can only talk to them at specified times; also my cell phone was taken when I checked in. It seems that our day was programmed for us, probably as much to prevent problems from patients with nothing to do. After breakfast every morning we went through this same routine; at this time we were also allowed to ask questions and supposedly get answers. Questions like why can I only use the phone at certain times of the day? Why can't I have a pen to write with only a pencil? Why can we only watch TV at specific times of the day? Why can my family visit only an hour a day at a specific time, often a time they can't get to the hospital because of work? The answer to most of these questions was "because those are the rules." The next question was why is that a rule, and there was no answer to that question. At this point it was beginning to dawn on me that I was not in a hospital but a prison; the only way out that I could see was to do exactly what I was told to do.

The first "class" of the day was called "group therapy". The staff randomly divided us into two groups. This seems to be the only piece of luck I had as I was placed in the group headed by the only person in the whole place that actually tried to help me, the only person who ever gave a damn about what happened to me. He was one of the social workers and he facilitated the "group therapy". In group we were all supposed to talk about what was happening in our lives and what had brought us to the hospital. First of all I didn't know any of these people around me. I felt decidedly unsafe and I was supposed to bare all, as if at this point I even knew what brought me here. I sat in the corner listening to people tell their stories. Some of them were horrific to listen to then it was my turn to tell my story. I just sat there. I was supposed to talk but I did not know what to say. So I said I was there because I tried to kill myself with an overdose of antihistamine. The minute that falls out of my mouth I know that's not the truth or at least not all of it; however, I didn't know what else to say. I didn't know anything except I felt scared and sad and desperate and I didn't know why. At this point I started to cry because that's all I could do to communicate my feelings. I cried the whole time or else I just sat huddled in the corner saying nothing and trying to hold myself together. After two and half hours of this therapy we returned to the day room for lunch. I spent the whole break time sitting in the corner again I was not hungry for food and then lunch was followed by another round of pills.

After lunch the next "group" was coping skills. This class consists of talking about your problems followed by the instructor and group members telling you ways to cope as if they really know you and what you are going through and have better coping skills. The instructor was unable to control the group and it turned into a shouting match. I absolutely hated this class. The only coping I got out of this torture was to learn to shut up and not get noticed, something I was already very good at. The last group was recreation skills. As if I needed a class to teach me to play games or draw. I taught this class to my multi-handicapped students.

Then all of a sudden a light bulb went off and I got it. There was something wrong with me that I previously knew nothing about. There must be something wrong with my brain. After all I now needed everyone to tell me what to do. I now needed all of those pills and now I needed a class to learn how to play games. I really must be brain damaged. I wandered to my room and lay down and cried myself to sleep while holding on to my pillow for dear life. I was adrift, I had no anchor, I did not know what was happening to me. I just kept sinking deeper into the dark and there was no light at the end of the tunnel. Surely I would wake from this nightmare soon. I jerked awake when the tech came down the hall announcing it was time for dinner. No, this was not a nightmare this was now my life. I didn't know why I should even get up, I did not want to eat no one would miss me. However, that was not in the program. I had to at least get up and go take more pills. I took my pills like a good little girl then wandered into the day room and found my plate. I nibbled then just sat staring.

Finally the highlight of my day came; visiting hour. My younger sister came; I don't remember what we talked about. I do know I did not really discuss how I felt or about trying to kill myself. It was as if, to me anyway, talking about real feelings at this point was too dangerous. After she left I took some more pills and cried myself to sleep again. Sleep did not last long as my body pain wakes me frequently. I went down the hall and found the day room was locked so I just sat in the hall. It seemed as if one day ran into the next that my main job was to become just sitting and staring or crying. Each morning my psychiatrist visits me; this consists of me sitting while he reads what others wrote about me. He would ask how I was feeling, at first being an honest person I would answer with the truth. I felt sad and cried all the time. He would ask me if I felt safe to which I would answer no.

Little did I realize those responses would prove to be the exact wrong thing to say. Because I told my doctor that I was sad and cried all the time, he of course upped the dosage of my medications. When I told him I did not feel safe he assumed I meant I would harm myself so my lock down on the unit continued. In fact when I answered that no I do not feel safe, I meant I felt decidedly unsafe in that hospital environment. I was still so confused about what had happened to me and what was still happening that I felt very unsafe. I was in an unfamiliar environment with people I did not know and who all felt unsafe to me. At that time I had no way of knowing that my actions of attempted suicide and my confusion and anxiety was largely due to a reaction to medication.

When I attempted "suicide", I did not see my actions as such until they were described to me in those terms. I had been taking Paxil for some time and had no idea of the side effects. Paxil, as I later found out, has been proven to increase suicidal ideation, a fact that was never explained to me before or after I became ill. In fact, the FDA did not even push the manufacturer to add that warning until 2006 long after I was under the drug's influence. The manufacturer, however, knew this to be a side effect for many years before the warning began being issued. Then while in the hospital, my psychiatrist took me off Paxil and started me on Zoloft, which has the same side effects, and he added a whole list of additional medications each with their own list of side effects and contra indications for taking with other medications, none of which I knew at the time.

The thing is when you are under the influence of those types of drugs even if you knew the side affects you are often unable to notice those effects in yourself. Anti-depressants, mood stabilizers, and tranquilizers are all brain disabling; that is in fact how they are intended to work. They affect your body, mind and soul so much so you have little if any idea what you are doing or saying. You behave in ways that you would never act if you were able to use your rational mind. In the end I could not even remember most of what had happened to me or what I had done. Eventually after having been on this mixture of drugs for a few of days I guess, I was compliant enough or said or did the right things and I was allowed to go with the group to eat and go outside twice a day. After a few more days of this "caring treatment" I was allowed to go home and the following Monday I returned to work as if nothing had happened to me at all.

One thing that sticks out in my brain that my psychiatric experience took from me was my joy in my work. It was after my mother died that I was able to complete my Bachelors in Special Education and so my career began much later in life than most, but I loved what I was doing and was good at it. My specialty was life skills. I worked with the children with the severest physical and developmental delays. Most were multi-handicapped and some had severe social and behavioral challenges as well. Not many people choose to work with this group of students and even fewer are very good at it. As I say I returned to work under the influence of all of these drugs. I could not tell you if I behaved differently though looking back on it I must have. I certainly felt differently. I remember feeling like a robot just going through the motions of living. To this day I could not tell you what students I had the last semester I taught. I cannot tell you what I taught or if I did a good job. No longer was teaching the joy it was to me before. Remembering what I can from that time I feel so cheated I get angry all over again. I was so muddled and sad it was all I could do to go through the motions of living. In order to survive I had to keep my job and to do that I had to force myself to turn off my emotions and pretend they weren't there. Of course the medication I was taking helped me stuff my emotions away. If asked what I was feeling, I do not know what I would have said but it is unlikely that I would have been able to tell you my true feelings. The bad part of not dealing with what was bothering me was that I began to feel so much worse, emotionally and physically. I just soldiered on until it literally became so awful to be me I could not deal with it.

That point came again for me in October of 2004 when I went to my medicine cabinet and took 20 or 30 Tylenol. My younger sister came home a few minutes later and I admitted what I had done. She took me to the emergency room at which time I had to drink about a gallon of charcoal and was later sent over to Shoal

Creek again. I went through the same checking in process and talking to various intake personnel about what was going on with me. This time I was feeling even worse than before so what information I could give had to be as confused as I was. This stay again included the changing of medications and upping of doses only to be released 5 days later with "maximum benefit" reached. This last I read from what records of mine I was able to obtain from the treating hospital. Someone really needs to explain the meaning of that statement to me. If that means I am more compliant and not complaining I guess that is maximum benefit. Or is it just the maximum amount of time in the hospital my insurance company was willing to pay for? I still don't know. By this time I was so heavily medicated that I would do good to tell you my name and yet when I was released I again returned to work.

My coping skills by this time were wearing thin and even my supervisors noticed. There were days I couldn't even get out of bed to go to work. At this point I think my spirit finally broke and I felt in real danger of killing myself. Of course little did I know my worsening psychologically and physically was largely due to drugs combined with real physical problems. Every time I went to the hospital the staff doctor did a physical exam and took blood and urine samples for tests. These tests are done to see if you have any underlying health issues that cause or contribute to emotional problems. The tests also check to see if the drugs they are giving you are causing health issues as well. According to the tests they took not only were my thyroid and blood sugar levels off (thyroid low and sugar high), but my potassium level had become seriously low and I was anemic due to blood in my urine, both things due to the drugs I was taking. I personally was never given these results. Any one of the afore mentioned results can and do cause emotional upsets such as what I was experiencing. The only thing Dr. Lam told me was that my potassium was very low and I was given supplements. None of the other results was ever mentioned. In fact I had no idea what they were testing for. When my potassium dipped so low and they found blood in my urine any reasonable practitioner should immediately reduce dosages of those drugs that caused the problems. Instead of lowering the medications that caused the metabolic unbalances they raised the dosages and added more salt to injury. In addition, if the blood sugar and thyroid issues had been dealt with right there and then perhaps my emotional problems would have stabilized as well.

Having none of this information I continued to take all of the <u>very expensive</u> medications and continued to work. Then while in the hospital for the third time in just a couple of months Dr. Lam suggested I apply for disability. My psychiatrist had convinced me that a normally functioning independent professional had suddenly and inexplicably become mentally ill and unstable. As my condition worsened, instead of looking at underlying causes and medication poisoning I was the one to blame for my illness. I could never be taken off of these healing pills because I was "Bi-Polar". Someone who had functioned independently for 47 years with no indication of mental instability was suddenly mentality ill and could never again be trusted to take care of herself or anyone else for that matter. Being that I was taught to be the compliant sort I bought everything that I was told hook, line and sinker. It is hard to believe that a rational human being would buy this line, but here's the thing under the influence of the drugs I was anything but rational. Those types of drugs are specifically designed to cause brain dysfunction. This suddenly became a totally life altering event and not even in a remotely good way.

During this same period my family's lives were drastically changing as well. My father was becoming more ill and unable to care for himself so my sisters and I as well as a good friend were taking turns caring for my dad at his apartment. My older sister lost the mobile home that she and her sons were living in with my dad and had to move to an apartment near my father. It is amazing to me as I look back on that period of time how easily and quickly my life came unraveled. How easy it is to undo a perfectly healthy mind. If you look at the brain it is covered with all of these intricate folds of matter. Looking at a brain reminds me of a labyrinth, how it folds back and forth on itself. Standing at the entrance it looks like simple design easily understood, but in reality it is a very complex part of our body that we as yet are only beginning to understand. This delicate beautiful machine runs and helps control all of the various parts of our body, including our mind. Why is it then that we think that we can control our mind and feelings with chemicals that destroy the brain, the very vehicle in which resides all of our thoughts and feelings. Why can we not see that these things destroy us rather than heal?

I ask myself that question a lot since my life unraveled. What I do know is I could not see that while under the influence of these drugs. So, where to begin the process of unraveling my life? I needed guidance, but who to contact? What to do? How do I receive social services? The first step was to talk with my younger sister and with my employer. As it turns out I did find one unlikely angel in the form of my helpful social worker at the hospital. As you can imagine unraveling one's life is a very difficult and emotional thing. Add to the mix all the other changes going on in my life and you have a recipe for disaster. At this time I was so drugged I could not remember anything from one moment to the next so the hospital gave me a composition book. This book became my constant companion and my only confessor. When I was discharged from the hospital, again with "maximum benefit achieved," I went home to begin taking apart my life.

Descent

Today
Part I

Today I will choose…
What enters me
What becomes one with my, body, mind and spirit.

Before without a true understanding
"True Informed Consent"
I became another guinea pig
To the psychiatric system
No more will I blindly accept
The word of the psychiatric system as law.

My body, mind, and spirit are not yours
For experimentation
With pills and mind/brain
Altering electric convulsive therapy.
Because I allowed this to happen
When I needed help
My situation is worse than before.

I am treated differently than I was before
Before I was a teacher
I helped deaf students with special needs.
Before I had a home
Before I was involved in the community
Before I had the support
Of many friends and family.

Now I have very little memory of my decline.
I can no longer work or drive.
I easily become lost,
My memory of my past has lots of gaps.
My short term memory is very short.
I now have few friends.
I am not the person I was before,
I am lost.

Today I choose…
To stand up and say to anyone who will listen.
To the law makers of the city, state
And federal governments.
These practices must stop
Especially electro convulsive therapy.

This is my body, mind and spirit.
I gave it to the psychiatric community
When I needed help.
I want it back.
My body mind and spirit
Are a non-negotiable demand.

Chapter Three

A Shocking Development

The brain- and mind-disabling hypothesis states that the more potent somatic therapies in psychiatry, that is, the major tranquilizers, lithium, ECT, and psychosurgery, produce brain damage and dysfunction, and that this damage and dysfunction is the primary, clinical or so-called beneficial effect. The individual subjected to the dysfunction becomes less able and more helpless, ultimately becoming . . . more suggestible or easy to influence.

Peter R. Breggin (1936-) "Disabling the Brain with Electroshock" In Maurice Dongier and Eric D. Winkower, eds., *Divergent Views in Psychiatry*, 1981(1)

It was during my last hospitalization that my psychiatrist convinced me that I was disabled unable to ever work or live on my own again. Where to begin the process of unraveling my life? I needed guidance. Who to contact? What to do? How do I receive needed disability services? What services are available to me? As you can imagine unraveling one's life is a very difficult emotional thing and confusing at the best of times. Add to the mix all the other changes in my life and you have a recipe for disaster. At this time I was so drugged that I could not remember anything from one moment to the next. Since I had no memory someone at the hospital gave me a composition book in which to write all the things I wanted and needed to remember. Since that time I have carried a book like that and the problem was I had to be repeatedly reminded to write things in my book and to read it several times a day. This is the only way I was able to function on a daily basis.

Since I was now suddenly disabled for the rest of my life with no hope of ever recovering I went to my supervisor after I got out of the hospital and informed her that I would be leaving my position after the holidays, never to teach again. One day I just went to my classroom and packed up my desk and a few personal things. I left the rest of ten years' worth of work and my entire school library. I remember my assistant (who that was I don't remember) came to tell me goodbye while I was packing. I shut my feelings about this ending of my career away and forced myself not to think about that passage until my writing of it here. At the time I refused to deal with those feelings or I would not have gotten through it. Now as I write I realize I gave away most of the things I had made for my classroom and the library I had built because to take it with me and store it away in my garage never to be used again was too awful to contemplate. It was the death of my dream I had worked for more than 15 years and I could not deal with the loss. Today almost six years later the grief is still very real for me. I packed my few personal things along with my grief and walked out of my classroom never to look back again and went home to celebrate the holiday with my family.

I am sure it is no big surprise that in January of 2005 I was again back in Shoal Creek hospital. This time I was so overwhelmed that I could not even function. This stay at the hospital lasted about a month. I was desperately unhappy and desperate to get away from my feelings. Instead of taking an overdose of pills, which my family carefully monitored, I cut my wrists. As with all of these incidents I was feeling so overcome with emotion and I had no way to communicate what I was feeling, so I felt I had no other choice because there was no way I was going to go on forever feeling that much hurt.

This time it did not matter what drugs the psychiatrist gave me; nothing helped. I wandered the halls of the hospital like a ghost caught between one world and the next needing a guide to find my way out. The only activities that I would engage in were working crossword and jigsaw puzzles. These activities did not require me to engage with anyone around me so they seemed safe and kept my hands and sometimes my mind busy. I attended all of their groups and classes but only sat like a stone or else cried through the whole thing. When not involved in one of these activities I would go to my room and sleep. I ate very little and would either sleep a lot or not at all. My pain, both emotional and physical, was so great that nothing could touch it.

I look back now and realize that the feelings of grief I had stuffed away related to the loss of my career on top of all of my other problems were too much for one person to bear alone. yet all who interacted with me pretended the elephant was not in the room. Being that I was not dealing with my feelings of grief, combined with the fact that the only help I was given was drugs on top of drugs, it's no wonder I felt so desperately alone. I felt like no one understood anything about me or what I was feeling. I was unable to understand what was causing my distress or find a way to get away from my grief. The doctors and staff knew I was not improving and only sinking further into a pit of despair. Even my one ally, the social worker at the hospital, was unable to reach me. I had sunk to my lowest point. Even after the death of my mother to breast cancer I had not felt this hopeless. The psychiatrist kept changing and adding various drugs, all with the promise that they would eventually find the right combination of drugs to help me. Eventually even my psychiatrist recognized that the drugs were not helping. What came next made everything that happened before seem inconsequential.

My memories from this point are literally almost totally wiped clean. So to say who suggested the next "form" of treatment next is unclear. What did happen was that the psychiatrist told me the drugs weren't working and the only course of treatment left to me was ECT or electroshock therapy. He told me that it was painless and the only side effects "might" be memory loss around the treatment time but that would return soon after. He explained that for someone who was so hopelessly depressed and drugs did not work this was the only treatment option left. I was led to believe that I would fully recover from the effects and would go on to live a happy healthy life. In addition a close friend told me she had gone through six or seven of these treatments and they had "cured" her depression. This, of course, is the company line given to all who undergo these treatments. The "cure", for some, is a disruption of the brain's ability to think and remember the problems they were faced with at the time. For most people it does not help at all (myself included), only hurts, or the effects are short term and have to be repeated in many cycles. As I was at the end of my rope and had no other recourse, or so I thought (after all the psychiatrist would not recommend anything that was harmful) I agreed to the treatments. The first couple of treatments were given to me while I was still in the hospital. Evidently the results were what the doctors had hoped for because after those treatments I was sent home with "maximum benefit achieved". Never mind that I have absolutely no memory of those treatments or of returning home.

Starting the next week I was to receive three ECT treatments a week. I do have some memories of arriving for those first few appointments. The electroshock treatments were and still are given at Shoal Creek Hospital where I stayed previously, although on a different floor. My older sister took me to most of my appointments as she worked at night. We arrived and were greeted by the R.N. who helped run the unit. This same nurse several years later became depressed and tried to commit suicide and she was given the same treatments I was. She is now on disability and unable to work or go places alone but she says she is now healthy. Each time we arrived in the waiting room, which was filled with typical chunky state bought furniture, there were often two or three persons waiting for treatment. Each person who came for treatment had a companion with her I say her because I never saw a man there, to see them safely home. After a treatment you could not be trusted to find your way home, if you even remembered who you were or even where home was. You could not even be left alone for a period of time after each procedure because there was no telling what you might do or where you might wander off to. Hell, you might even have another seizure and no one would know about it, least of all yourself. After arriving I would sign in and my sister and I would wait for the nurse. One thing that occurs to me is that no matter how many other people were waiting we never talked to each other or even looked into one another's eyes. It was as if we felt shamed by what we were doing.

A few minutes after we arrived the nurse would come in and give me pills to take before the procedure. At first I was given just a couple of pills and was told they were for reflux. Later more pills were added but I was told the same thing. Each time I came for treatment I was given a stack of consent papers to sign and, just as when I went into the hospital, I signed them all. I am just guessing here but they probably told me what each of the forms were that I was consenting to before my first treatment in the hospital. However, on subsequent visits, some of which I remember, the nurse just pointed to each place to sign and I complied. One thing I do remember reading is that I was told not to sign or make contracts for several days after the treatment, yet each time I was given this complex contract to sign. These consents are important to the doctors and hospital as they are proof that I consented to everything that they did to me. I do remember that the consents and procedures were never explained to me by a doctor only by nurses and attendants at the hospital. I still contend that I did not have fully informed consent to the procedures; after all the doctors never told me that each time I went through the treatment they would have to increase the amount of shock both in intensity and duration. Also they flat out lied about my memory loss and returning to normal functioning. Plus my state of mind was severely disordered by all the drugs.

The nurse then left us to wait until the pills took effect, then I was led back into the treatment room. Each time I was asked to remove my shoes and all of my jewelry and glasses. After going through this procedure I turned toward the gurney where I was to lie. I saw two doctors next to it and behind them the "machine" which would run electricity through my brain. My first thought was of a sci-fi movie where there was a panel on the wall with all of these dials and knobs like Doctor Frankenstein used. After I lay down the doctor at the head of the table, who was an anesthesiologist, administered the oxygen and anesthesia. He would place an oxygen mask over my nose and mouth while I was strapped to the table and the rails were raised so I would not fall or hurt myself. He always had me count backward from 100 and told me to relax. After that point my memory is a total blank. I have no memory of waking up or going home or anything for days prior to or after a treatment.

In between treatments I was at first going to group therapy at the hospital until I was told I was too empathetic to continue. I have no idea what they meant by that except a comment about me crying and unable to stop. Instead of improving I was worsening. After about three weeks I again found myself in the hospital having taken an overdose of ibuprofen. Evidently the doctors had yet to find the right combination of drugs and electroshock therapy. It was during this hospitalization that two more life changing events occurred that finally pulled the last moorings from my formerly stable life.

My father had become increasingly unable to care for himself and fell one night and hit his head on the bedside table. My sister went to check on him and found he had hurt himself and was ill as well. She took him to the emergency room and the hospital admitted him. The doctors found he again had an intestinal infection and that he had also had a small stroke. Both of my sisters convinced him and his doctor that he could not go home to live alone again. So he was placed in a local nursing facility. In essence I was not able to be there for my father when he needed me most.

Secondly, sometime during all of this upheaval going on in me and my family's lives, my younger sister with whom I lived and one of our best friends began a relationship. This in itself would not have upset me. Both of them were happier than I have seen either of them; the problem was they wanted to live together as partners and wanted to ask me to move out. As this relationship had developed while I was in the hospital I had no idea what was happening. They evidently had a meeting with my psychiatrist and both him and my older sister wanted them to wait to tell me and ask me to move. They did not wish to wait or hide their intentions any longer so proceeded to set up a family meeting to tell me while I was still in the hospital and with my psychiatrist present. If they had waited to tell me and I found out they had hidden all of this from me I would have felt even more betrayed. In the end no matter how it played out I still felt abandoned and betrayed.

My sister and I had picked out the house together and were paying for it together, so naturally I considered it half my home as well. When my sister and I bought the house five years before, my credit was bad so the house was bought in her name and I had no legal say as to what happened to it. Since then she and I had been paying for everything together until I quit my job in December. For the last couple of months she had been paying for everything and could not continue to do so. The home my sister and I were buying and living in had no equity built up. If she sold the house she would end up still owing on it. However, her partner owned her own house which she sold in order to move in with my sister. I was then asked to move out when I got my disability and had funds to do so. Since my sister and I were paying for the house together I considered it my home and they, in my view had no right to ask me to move with no consideration for what I had put into it. It was my home along with my sister and yet because I was suddenly unable to work it was no longer mine. They were willing to let me stay until I was able to get my own place. While I understand the bind my sister was in, it seemed no consideration was made for what I had lost and was continuing to lose due to no fault of my own. I was angry and felt abandoned and betrayed on top of the grief I was feeling about the loss of my career.

During this time frame my social worker friend was helping me apply for my disability. No matter how many physical problems I had in my life, such as arthritis and fibromyalgia, I never saw myself as disabled. For 20 years I had worked with individuals with all kinds of physical and intellectual problems, but I never considered myself disabled in any way. Sure I had chronic physical problems but nothing I was unable to work around. Now I was facing all of these emotional problems and labels such as bi-polar, severe depression, and even personality disorder. Add to that the fact that I had no idea of how to cope with all of these new "illnesses."

To listen to my doctor say it, the only hope I had was drugs and electroshock. These illnesses could never be cured, only treated. Suddenly I am now unable to work or even care for myself sometimes in the most basic of ways. Just to be told that this is all I had to look forward to for the rest of my life was overwhelming, not to mention the process of dealing with the government and all of their red tape. The first time I applied for disability I was denied. I think this is probably an automatic as a matter of practice to weed out people who are not very determined. After that I had to file an appeal in which they asked for all kinds of proof of my disability. I was by this time unable to even fill out all of the paperwork by myself and my younger sister and my social worker friend helped with this process. Eventually I was asked to come to the social security office to undergo competency testing. This was during the time I was also receiving ECT.

My older sister took me to a big federal office building somewhere downtown. When I think back to the few things I remember during this time it seems to me as if I was moving in a dark fog. It was as if I was in this dark cloudy dream like state and only occasionally did the fog lift enough for me to see some of my surroundings. In this federal building I was taken to a glass cubicle where a couple of women administered their test. I believe the test took a couple of hours; the flow of time was as amorphous as the rest of my memories. These women asked me about my life. They also asked questions like, name the current president, name all of your friends and family and their phone numbers and addresses, and tell me how to get to your house from here. I tell people that at times I would leave my home to go to the mail box and could not find my way home or at time not remember my own name. Most people think I am exaggerating, but truly I am not. At that time, however, you had to be unemployed for six months before social security disability started. Even at that they would only begin payments to me if I had a guardian to take care of my money. Evidently I could not be trusted to do even that much and at that time they were right. The strange thing is not one person, myself included, ever considered that this was due to drugs and not any real disability.

The number of people having to be put on disability has risen drastically since psychiatry began treating emotional problems with drugs as a matter of course. In fact most of the people on disability have had to do so because of the drugs that their psychiatrists insist they have to take. What if instead of drugging people we gave them a safe place to talk about their problems? That way people can work out their problems and we can drastically reduce the number of people who are forced to use state and federal funds to live. A lot of the people I have seen stuck in this system have little recourse and it is a difficult proposition at best to get out of it.

In July of 2005 I was set to start receiving SSDI of about $1000 a month, which is more than most people get on disability. I would also eventually receive Medicare, but only after I had been out of work for two years. At first I kept my insurance from work through Cobra, but as the payments were almost $800 a month that quickly became an impossible task. I had no choice but to take my retirement money out of my account and use that to live on. I guess I was competent enough to do that, although perhaps I should have had some guidance in that area as well. After taxes I was awarded about 10,000, which sounds like a lot but in reality does not go far. I believe I paid on my bills though I can't be sure how much. I also bought new appliances and things for the house I was living in with my little sister. As to what happened to the rest of it I don't know. I am sure I was the one who spent it but on what I could not say. In a couple of months my money was gone. My younger sister, with whom I was living, was frustrated with my behavior and spending at this time. To her it probably seemed I was just being irresponsible and as if I did not care what problems I was causing. Having been on the flip side of that situation now I can tell you I was not thinking at all. The truth is while under the influence of drugs and electroshock there is no way I could reason anything through. I understand that. To the person not on drugs it looks like your behavior is deliberately irresponsible. If someone were talking with me about specific subjects I probably sounded as if I knew what I was doing. However, now that I am truly clear headed I can tell you I had no idea what I was doing or saying.

So I was deemed disabled and unable to even care for my own money. I was still living at home with my younger sister and her partner and as soon as my money came I was to start looking for a place of my own. Believe it or not, at the same time I was declared unable to take care of my own money I was still considered able to decide everything else for myself and was still driving myself around except for the days I had electroshock treatments.

My driving did not, however, continue for very much longer. I remember one day driving home with my older sister from some place and I drove over the line several times and over curbs two or three times. When my sister asked me about it I told her it was all I could do to focus on one thing at a time, much less the multiple tasks you need to perform to drive safely. The incident that stopped my driving altogether happened a couple of weeks later. My older sister, who works as a home health nurse, got stranded one night on the way home from work. She called my house and asked to be picked up. I don't remember why, but I was sent to get her. It was about 8 or 9 pm and in an unfamiliar part of town. Evidently I became disoriented and got lost. I had no phone and I don't remember if I even had any money. After about an hour my older sister again called my home to see where I was. At this point everyone got concerned and my younger sister and her partner got in their car to go pick up my older sister. In the meantime I found my way to a convenience store and was able to call home. The store owner was able to tell them where I was so they could come get me. To this day I have no idea where I was. After that my older sister took my vehicle and started making the payments. I had paid all but about one year of the loan, now I had no car. One more thing I was now unable to do for myself that my family had to start doing for me.

As the weeks went by and my treatment continued my situation at home deteriorated. I was slowly losing everything that once made up the bulk of my life. Gone were my career, job and income, along with the meaning those things brought to my life. I defined a great portion of myself by my career. I was and am a teacher, and yet I would, according to my psychiatrist, never be able to define myself that way again. As of that moment I could not drive or even take care of my money or my own medicine. I had suddenly become as disabled as many of the students I had served. Yet it seemed not to occur to anyone around me, or myself, that something was fundamentally wrong with this picture. In addition I was at war with myself about my home situation. Anyone who knew me then would tell you that I would literally have rather cut off an arm than be angry with or hurt the feelings of someone I cared about. There is no doubt I loved both my sister and her partner, but at the same time I was so angry about being asked to leave my own home that I did not know what to do. If I expressed my anger I was sure my sister would stop loving me and I would rather die than face that situation. Yet at the same time I blamed myself for everything that was happening. It had to be my fault otherwise none of these events would be happening to me. As I write of these events, I know these are the feelings I had internalized, but at that time I could not have articulated any of this. I just felt more and more betrayed and angry and had no way to express my feelings except to take it out on myself. To do anything else would cost me too much. I have since reread notes made in my journal by me and others that urged me to resolve this conflict with my sister so I could heal. However, I was so afraid of losing the love of anyone I cared about that I could not bring myself to do this. The situation became so utterly toxic for me that when my older sister suggested I move into her two bedroom apartment that I jumped at the chance and began making preparations to move out. My little sister and I had been almost inseparable from the time she came home from the hospital when I was five years old. She and I had lived together as adults from the time of my divorce 20 years before. We used to joke that when we divorced, my sister and I, that one would get custody of this or that, but now I was faced with the reality of that very situation. I had already lost so much in the last few months that the dividing of actual physical things became very overwhelming to me. The loss of each thing felt like a theft. As a result I ended up resenting the loss of each object even if it was not really of great importance to me. It would be a long time before I was able to actually let go of things that did not serve me after that.

Pressure
I feel pressure building
Pressure of emotions fighting to escape
They need to come out
They need an escape and yet
Like a pressure cooker with a bad valve
I fear they will escape and burn who ever
I come into contact with.

In fear of this I retreat
Into my lonely room
Into my ever shrinking world
Into myself
But the pressure is still there.
Now they are not just bubbling but
Erupting out of me in great waves of grief.
Yet I don't want to burden others so I clutch my pillow
To muffle the sounds.

These feelings are too much for me to bear.
I can't live with them inside me any more
They tear out of me ripping a hole in my soul and yet
They continue to come in great waves

I don't want these feelings anymore.
I need someone to hold me and comfort me
Yet I have no one there
This must be of my doing or
I would not be suffering so.
A glimmer of light shines on the blade of a knife
Lying on the bedside table…
What if you use me to cut yourself?
It seems to say to me
What a strange thought but
Oddly comforting as
I pick up the blade and hold it in my hand.

I lie the sharp side next to my skin and
Feel its steely coolness
As I consider the thought.
Do you think it will relieve the pressure
Inside if you cut?
I grit my teeth and make a hesitant first cut
It barely makes a mark
For all the sharp pain coming out
So again and again I slice
Deeper and deeper still.
Each stroke causing more pain to be released.
Then finally starts the blood
At first a trickle
Later a steady flow.
I lie watching the flow of blood
Running down my arm.
It's oddly comforting
Eventually
I fall asleep
With blood drying on my arm
And tears drying on my face.
The valve has been released…
At least till I wake
To find the feelings there…
Still.

Chapter 4

Death of Self

[After the shock treatment] I rise disembodied from the dark to grasp and attach myself like a homeless parasite to the shape of my identity and its position in space and time. At first I cannot find my way, I cannot find myself where I left myself, someone has removed all trace of me. I am crying. Janet Frame (1924-), Faces in the Water, 1,1, 1961(1)

Most memories of the following time period have been erased from my mind as if they had never happened. However, I have found in my journal lists of things I was planning to bring with me when I left what is now my younger sister and her partner's home. I don't even recall when it really sunk in that I was essentially homeless and yet from journal entries I know on some level I was aware of what was happening. The trouble was that every time I had another shock treatment I would forget all over again. It's kind of like that movie, Fifty First Dates, where the actress woke every morning to think it was a specific day with no memory of what came after that actual date. Each night she went to sleep she forgot all over again what had just happened and awoke to think she was living the previous date again. To keep any memory of what was going on I had to write everything down and constantly reread it. I don't know if my family just got tired of repeating to me why I had to move or if they felt I was accusing them of something every time I asked about it, probably both. Eventually they just stopped talking to me about it.

While I can guess at the pain and frustration my family was going through I can't say for sure what their true feelings were. I only know I was lost in a fog of pain and loss I did not know how to get out of it. In the middle of all of this confusion I have one very clear memory. It must have been the day I moved in with my older sister. I have one very clear snapshot of memory from that day.

It was a bright sunny summer day. My oldest nephew, my older sister and I were moving my bed down the stairs to her apartment and setting my bed up in her second bedroom. This room became not only my bedroom but pretty much my whole world. I distinctly remember setting up the bed with the headboard under the only window in the room. It was sunny and hot and everyone was cranky because of the heat combined with the stress of moving. The rest of that move is now gone from my memory forever.

At the time, even my psychiatrist felt moving was the best thing for me, but I can now say living in such small quarters with so many people nearly undid me and my whole family. First of all my oldest nephew was already living with his mother and gave up his room for me. Now he only had the living room for his living quarters, no privacy there, and we shared the bathroom on my side of the apartment. To make matters worse a few months later my younger nephew, who had been working and living in San Francisco, also returned to live with us. He now shared the living room with his brother. My older nephew slept in the recliner and my younger nephew slept on a fold up cot. Even though my nephews were adults and only planned to live there a short time they could not have been happy with the situation.

By this time my older sister had accepted the additional responsibility of taking me everywhere I needed to go as well as running the house and keeping a more than full time job. My nephews tried to find work

Evelyn Scogin

but were less than successful so we mainly depended on my sister for support with what help I eventually was able to give when I started receiving my SSDI checks. All in all it was a poor solution to a very bad situation, but one we did not know how to get out of and so we muddled through as best we could. I know I kept my bedroom and bathroom clean and did my own laundry. As far as the rest of the chores I probably helped with them when I was able but don't really remember doing so. By this time I was unable to go anywhere alone, for fear of becoming disoriented and lost. I spent most of my time in my room reading or watching TV. My once full and meaningful life was reduced to four walls and a television set.

One more important thing happened when I moved in with my older sister. While living with my younger sister I had a dog, two cats and a guinea pig, a school pet. When I moved I did bring my guinea pig and cats with me. As my dog was a very large breed I did not immediately move her with me for fear she would not adapt well to the limited environment of the apartment when she had previously been used to a large yard to run in. Then in about September of that year my younger sister said my dog was missing me horribly so I decided to move her in with me. This turned out in one way to be a good thing. Because she needed walking it required me leaving my room for short periods of time several times a day. Then in October my dog became ill and when I took her to the vet he found she was in the last stages of cancer. I could not stand the thought of my beloved companion being in pain and I could ill afford the vet bills so I decided to put her to sleep. Then the next week my older sister's apartment management found out I had two cats and my sister already had two, which was the limit. I had to then find a no kill shelter and by the end of that week my cats were gone as well. I do vividly remember saying good bye to

63

my beloved dog at the vet and next week having to say good bye to my cats as well. The shelter had an open day room for the cats to roam in and I went in and sat on the floor and petted my two boys for the last time. The look of utter confusion and loss on their faces will haunt me for a long time. I now truly had nothing and, I felt, no one to live for.

I continued taking electroshock treatments two to three times a week as my emotional stability continued to deteriorate. During the time I was taking electroshock treatments my feelings of grief, fear and anger would build up and having no place else to go or any way to express them I began taking my feelings out on myself. I would find a sharp object, usually a box cutter or a piece of glass. I would go to my room and shut the door so no one would hear me. I turned off all of the lights in my room and lay on my bed and cried for hours. Inside I was screaming out my pain, but I did not want to bother anyone so I would cry into my pillow. Eventually my pain would be too much and I would start cutting myself. Since I am right handed I mostly cut my left forearm, but eventually I would cut both arms. I would grit my teeth and start with a shallow cut and then I would cut the same spot deeper and deeper until my blood began to flow. Even then I would continue cutting until the blood flowed freely down my arms.

In some way this released the emotional pressure I was feeling. Since being in therapy and learning to express my feelings in appropriate ways I realized my cutting was a valve. Like when you become very angry and you can't yell at the person or thing you need to yell at so you throw things or scream. At that time I could not bring myself to do any of those things because I was convinced that I was to blame for everything that had happened to me. I also believed that if I expressed my hurt and anger to the people I needed to I would lose their love forever and that was something I would not risk doing. I would cry and cut all alone in my room and all alone within myself until I fell asleep. My older sister would come to check on me and find me all cut up and bleeding. This would lead to another trip to the psychiatric hospital. I would stay for 5 to 7 days while my drug cocktail was changed and dosages ever increased. Then the electroshock would start all over again. The very doctors that were supposedly helping me instead were slowly poisoning and electrocuting me to death. My emotional health was declining; so my physical health.

Each of the drugs I was prescribed had its own side effects, not to mention interactions with each other. Most people are lead to believe, as was I, that the psychiatrists, doctors and pharmacists knew what the side effects and interactions are and keep up with each of them that you are taking so that you are never put into danger. The truth is people have side effects from drugs of all kinds all of the time and they are usually not recognized as that, especially if the effects are with someone who has a psychiatric diagnosis. For instance I began having hallucinations. I would tell my family I saw cats walking across the room or I would see snakes coming out of the trash cans. I don't actually remember seeing those things but no one myself, my family, or my psychiatrist attributed those things to drug side effects. Since doing some research about the drugs I was taking; I discovered that hallucinations were listed as a side effect of several of them. Yet even though I have never experienced hallucinations before or since getting off all of those drugs the psychiatrist just labeled me as bipolar with psychotic features instead of looking at the real cause of the problem. Another problem caused or exacerbated by the drugs and electroshock was that my thyroid stopped functioning correctly and I became even more overweight as well as diabetic. My arthritis and fibromyalgia became much worse and I developed psoriasis. I would have periods of insomnia followed by periods when I could not stay awake yet none of these effects were ascribed to the ever increasing amount of drugs I was taking.

The electroshock was having its effects as well. I had no short term memory and had lost a lot of my long term memory. I also became increasingly paranoid about going to my electroshock treatments. I would not leave my room and was afraid to be in a large group of people. Of course to deal with this issue my psychiatrist prescribed Klonopin, a drug supposedly for people with panic attacks.

During this time I had a dream or perhaps an out of body experience about these treatments. While floating above I saw myself lying on the table in the electroshock treatment room. I was strapped down to the table and the electrodes were attached to me and I saw the psychiatrist turn on the machine. My body began to convulse on the table. When the convulsions stopped the psychiatrist, anesthesiologist and nurse realized I had stopped breathing. They gave me CPR and I began breathing again. I never told anyone about that dream to this day, but after the dream or incident, or whatever it was? I became seriously scared of those treatments. My older sister told me that as the treatments progressed when they would release me to go home I was increasingly drugged and confused. In fact there were several times I was sent home when I was unable to walk from the hospital and had to be carried out by my sister leaning me on various walls to get to the elevator and then the car. My older sister is a nurse and she told me that no hospital should release a patient post op or treatment that could not stand on their own or was so confused they did not know where they were. Later I found out that at each treatment the amount of shock and drugs used on me were increased, all without either me or my sister being informed of these changes. At times the drugs and shock would cause me to urinate on myself during the treatment and I was sent home with my clothes soiled. They did not even try to help me change my clothes or clean me up first.

My family became increasingly worried about my mental and physical health while these treatments continued. They have since told me that they tried to convince me to stop the treatments. However, as I was still convinced that my psychiatrist would not order treatment that would harm me I continued the treatments. One day I finally admitted to my older sister how scared I was of these treatments, even though I did not actually remember them. She at that point reminded me that I had the right to stop the treatments anytime I wished. It took all of the courage I had at that time but eventually my fear of the continued treatments overcame my fear of over ruling my psychiatrist. I called his office and spoke to him and asked if I could stop treatments. He told me I could always stop treatment anytime I wished and that was the end of my shock treatments.

Since obtaining as many of my hospital records as the hospital would release to me I found out in a six month period I was given at least 31 shock treatments. More detailed information about my electroshock treatments is in the article *One Woman's Near Destruction and Reemergence from Psychiatric Assault: The Inspiring Story of Evelyn Scogin.* My ending of my shock treatments was a very important first step in my recovery. It might seem a small but logical thing to someone else, but for me to go against what the doctor had ordered was an enormous thing. It planted the seed that I could decide to follow the treatment the psychiatrist ordered or I could use my adult voice and say no I don't want that. Your treatment is not helping me and only making me worse. Still after that one bit of protest I again subsided to the compliant patient. After all I am not a doctor and if he said that I could never stop taking these drugs for the rest of my life I believed him.

Still as the months of living with my sister and her sons in this very small environment, continued now for more than a year, emotions for all of us became frayed. I tried to stay mostly in my room, but my erratic behavior began to take its toll on all of us. My nephews seeing only my outward behavior believed, as most people would, that I was only behaving this way to get attention. My youngest nephew called it passive aggressive behavior, a term that psychiatrists came up with to label some of the behaviors I was exhibiting and thus laying the blame for all I was feeling and doing completely at my door and doing nothing to find out why I was acting in such unusual ways.

One night I was having trouble sleeping so I decided to rearrange my bedroom. Rearranging the furniture in my house has for some odd reason been a kind of therapy for me. You can ask my older sister, from the time I was able to move the furniture in our bed room, probably about age 10, and I would at times of stress rearrange our room. So this night I could not sleep and was rearranging again. How I moved all of the furniture around in that room without moving it out into the hall is beyond me, but nevertheless that is exactly what I did. In order to move the bed I had to remove the mattress and box spring and stand them up against the wall. At this point I was so full of various drugs I could barely stand straight. While trying to move the bed frame I fell over the bed rail. This woke the whole household and they all came rushing in to see what had happened. I could not even get myself up off the floor. When they did manage to help me up I insisted on finishing moving my bed even though it was 4am and all of them had to go to work in a few hours. Naturally they were furious with me and I had no clue that I was being unreasonable. It must have been like dealing with an intoxicated person, which of course I was. The problem being I was intoxicated on drugs that were supposed to help me function and no one, myself included, blamed my behavior on the drugs. As I stated my nephews thought I was just trying to get attention. My poor sister just thought I was out of my mind, which of course I was, though not due to any biological illness, but instead due to drug intoxication.

The whole biopsychiatric system is set up to work in precisely this way. The psychiatrists convince you they are actually helping you. They convinced me, my family and the world in general that all of these so called "mental illnesses" are biologically based and have been proven by science. Nothing could actually be further from the truth. While there are actual illnesses that can effect emotional and behavioral changes, such as thyroid and blood sugar problems, in most cases there are a lot of factors that play into emotional problems. One thing I can tell you for sure drugs and electroshock are not designed to heal any emotional issues you have. They are only designed to disrupt the brain's ability to function properly. The only people these drugs are designed to help are the psychiatrists and pharmaceutical companies whose pockets are lined with money earned from them.

Another issue I began to have during this time was that I would go for a walk to the mailbox, about a block away at the apartment office, and I could not find my way back to the right apartment. I might actually get to the right building but since all the apartments looked the same I would try to get into the wrong apartment. Once I actually walked into an empty apartment and several times I tried my key in an apartment door only to find it did not fit. Several times my family had to come and find me as I was just wandering around trying to find the right apartment. They were literally afraid of what I might do if I wandered out of the house.

By this time my disability had kicked in but I had to wait another year for Medicare to start and as I could no longer pay for my cobra insurance, $800 a month, I had no way to pay to get my medicine or to see my doctors. My psychiatrist gave me free samples a couple of times, but eventually I had to stop seeing him as most private psychiatrists do not accept Medicare unless you have a secondary insurance. They want to get paid their full fee and not just what Medicare will pay. So I had no choice but to find free clinics. Having had no experience with getting social services I again turned to my friend at the psychiatric hospital and he told me about services through the city so that I could see a doctor and get prescriptions filled for a small amount. As for psychiatric help I had to go to the state run MHMR clinic.

Having experienced both private and public biopsychiatry I can tell you I know why there are a lot of people who live on the street and have been irreparably harmed and refused further help. While private psychiatrists will order all kinds of meds and electroshock if you have insurance coverage, you get dropped like a hot potato the minute your insurance runs out. The psychiatrists that work for MHMR are just as bad for many reasons. First they have so many people to see that they don't have time to really "see" you. As with the private psychiatrists they only devote 10 or 15 minutes to each person and then only to fill your prescriptions. There are no counselors to be had in that system. In that system you really are just a number.

They run hundreds through their clinic daily. To be honest they are not given the funds to hire enough people to have enough time to spend with each person. They only see you once every three months unless you have a "psychiatric crisis".

For people in crisis they have a whole other clinic open 24 hours a day and staffed with the most over worked and least caring people I have ever met. Truly if you have a real crisis you would be better off finding someone on the street to talk to. I remember once I went there when I had the guts to tell my sister's partner that I felt suicidal. She took me to this clinic and we sat there for hours before we were actually seen by the psychiatrist who was unlucky enough to be on duty that night. All of the people who were working there were behind locked doors and you only got to talk to them through a slot under a thick piece of glass. They handed me a clipboard with a stack of papers and a pen which I had to fill out in order to be seen. Remember I went there because I finally felt strong enough to say I needed help and please help me. I finally got in to see the psychiatrist at about 11pm. He asked me why I was there and I told him I was feeling suicidal. The first thing he tried to do was have me admit myself to the state mental hospital, which I refused to do. When I refused to do that he became very angry with me and said, then what is it you do want? Do you want more drugs? I won't give you any more drugs. I became angry back and said I only wanted help from him, not drugs, and not to be locked away in the state hospital. He then left the office and when he came back he said I would have to go the hospital or he would call the police and have me arrested. I was flabbergasted and yelled back that I would not go to the hospital and since he refused to help me I was going home. He said he had already called the police and if I did not stay and talk to them they would come to my house and arrest me and drag me to the state hospital.

Well I did not know what to say or do. He left the office and refused to even talk to me. I went back to the window and talked to the woman there. She told me he indeed had called the police, that it was the law. If I said I was suicidal and refused their "aid," then they had to call the police. The police would come and talk to me. In Austin I found out they have a specially trained set of officers to deal with mental patients. After I talked to the police they would decide if I had to be forced into the hospital or released to go home. Either way if I left without permission or without talking to the police they would arrest me and take me to the hospital without my permission. She further explained it was in my best interest to stay and talk to the police as they usually decided not to take the person to the hospital. Now I don't know what special training they had that qualified them to decide if I was a danger to myself or others but the receptionist indeed told me the truth. In a short time a trio of officers came to talk to me and took me into the psychiatrist's office. I don't remember what they asked me or what I said but evidently it satisfied them and they let me go. How anyone has a right to take my civil liberties away without due process and without me actually threatening myself or anyone else is beyond me. These people were serious and would have followed through with their threat; after all suicide is against the law. I don't as a citizen have a right to decide if I want to continue living or not. I came for help and this was what happened to me. I got no help, only threats to my civil liberties if I did not follow orders. Does this sound like what our forefathers set up in our constitution? You get constitutional rights unless you are considered a mental patient. Even someone accused of a crime has to have their civil rights assured, but evidently not me.

Having no other recourse I did continue to see my psychiatrist at the regular clinic in order to get my prescriptions filled. One good thing that did happen while I was seeing the psychiatrists there; I told my psychiatrist about my problems of getting lost and that since I lived with my older sister the apartment complex would not let me have a dog. He wrote a letter that allowed me to get a dog for companionship and to keep me from getting lost. The apartment complex then allowed me to keep a dog without paying a fee as the dog was certified a service animal. My sister's partner helped me get a dog that needed rescuing and I trained her to help me find my way to and from places. To this day my companion and I live together and take care of one another. She has several times prevented me from getting lost as well as one incredible incident when she went and got help for me when I fell.

Except for going for walks with my companion dog around the apartment complex I only left to go to various doctor's appointments or to visit my father with my family. My father by this time was living in a nursing home and one member of my family or another would arrange for me to go with them to visit him on a weekly basis. While on a visit one day my family and I noticed that one of the nurse aides had brought her dog with her. The dog and the patients both loved visiting with her and both benefited from it. That planted the idea in my head. My father had to give up his two pugs to move to the nursing facility and so I asked if I could occasionally bring my dog to visit. The only thing I had to do was prove she had current shots. So my sweet toy poodle and I began not only visiting my father but some of the other patients as well. This truly became one of the few bright spots in my limited life.

Even after I stopped taking the electroshock treatments my life did not drastically improve. I am writing a little now about some of the very few vivid memories I have of that time or ones I have since recovered after much therapy. Of those few things I do recall from my years since involvement with biopsychiatry, most are such that people would not want to remember. Things in my and my families' lives did not improve or change much as I continued the drug regimen prescribed for me unabated. I had no counselor and only went to see a psychiatrist to keep my prescriptions current. Meanwhile my physical and emotional health as well as the lives of my family continued to deteriorate. My nephews continued to feel resentment toward me and my behavior. No one understood my behavior least of all me. As I continued the drugs, my insomnia got worse so my psychiatrist in all of his wisdom changed me to a new long acting sleeping pill just out on the market. Little did I know that this pill would cause some of the strangest behavior changes I have ever experienced. One night I started sleep walking, something I did as a child. I got up one night and went into the kitchen and got a soda and a pint of ice cream then started back to my bedroom. I did not know I was half asleep and half hallucinating. As I was making my way back to my bedroom, silently I hoped, I walked into something in my way. To my brain I was walking into my bedroom through the doorway and I saw no obstruction. So, when I met an obstacle my brain processed it as my doorway and I kept trying to walk through it until I finally fell over what was actually my youngest nephew sleeping on his cot in the living room. I fell on top of him and my ice cream and soda flew everywhere. It took my brain a few moments to process what had actually happened. I bruised both me and him and my older nephew and my sister had to pick me up and put me to bed. It wasn't until the next day when the medication had worn off and I truly woke that I knew what had happened. It did not matter that I was sorry and apologetic about what had happened; my family did not understand that I did not know what I was doing. My youngest nephew stopped talking to me and started taking it out on me in ways that I mostly don't remember.

Then just a few days later I had another waking dream. This time I managed not to wake the household but came close to seriously hurting myself. I don't remember most of the dream but during this episode I managed to unlock the front door and climb up a set of stairs to the parking lot. In the dream I remember I kept trying to set down on a piece of furniture but I kept falling on the floor. In reality I was trying to sit down on a curb in the parking lot and kept falling to the ground. Eventually I stumbled back down stairs in my dream and back to my bed. The next day I found bruises all over my body and I had a big lump on the back of my head. My oldest nephew found the door open and unlocked. Only then did I remember the dream and figured out what had actually happened. This behavior scared me as nothing else had previously done. At that time I was truly in fear of losing my mind and did not tell my family what had happened. About this time things really spiraled out of control for all of us. Both of my nephews were unable to find more than temporary employment and this put a strain on everyone. They started having arguments with each other as well as the strain my behavior had already put on the family. Several times the police were called to our apartment to deal with these arguments. Of course being me, I secretly felt that most of their behavior was my fault.

Also during this time my Father's health continued to deteriorate. Family always came first with me and it was especially hard to visit my dad knowing that I was unable to be there for him when he really needed me. I was limited to going only on those days when I had a ride to the nursing home and could only stay as long as my family stayed. My father was bedridden and only able to move out of the bed with a lift. His favorite thing was to watch the birds outside his window. His roommate would scatter seeds on the ground under the tree outside his window every day and my sister got him a feeder that stuck to the outside of his window. I still put a red bird, my father's favorite, on my holiday tree each year in his honor. One visit sticks out in my mind during that time. My father asked me to please come one day and spend the whole day with him. He wanted me to watch his western movies with him and read to him, really just spend time with him. I told him I would try but as I had no way there or back except with my family, we both knew this was unlikely to happen. To this day I regret not finding a way to meet that simple request.

I suppose me and my family's lives could have continued on in this way forever if it had not been for several events that occurred one right after the other. These events not only brought things to a head, so to speak, but would irrevocably change the course my life was to take.

The Quality of Silence

All alone in my room I sat
Silent except for the noise of the television
My voice unheard
My feelings hidden even from myself
Forgotten by the community
I was once so much a part of
Drugged and shocked and
Closeted away in my room
Silenced and silent

Funny thing about silence
It only continues until
There is a sound to shatter it.
First it was just a whisper
Then it turned into a sob
Then a shout of anger
And now a clear strong voice
That will be silenced never more.
A voice that dares speak the truth
Of the abuses perpetrated upon her.
A voice that speaks
Not only for herself but
For those who have yet to
Or are just beginning to find their voices.
From one, to two,
To so many that
Our voices can no longer be ignored.
But it started from silence
And just my one small voice.

Descent

Chapter 5

A Chance Meeting

If institutional Psychiatry is harmful to the so-called mental patient, this is not because it is liable to abuse, but rather because harming persons categorized as insane is its essential function: Institutional Psychiatry is, as it were, designed to protect and uplift the group (the family, the State), by persecuting and degrading the individual (as insane or ill).Thomas Szasz (1920-), Hungarian-born American psychiatrist. *Introduction to The Manufacture of Madness: A Comparative Study of the Inquisition and the Mental Health Movement,* 1970(1)

It was just a chance meeting that changed the course of me and my family's lives. One day my older sister and my youngest nephew were hunting for a storage facility in which to place his things. I suggested a facility near our apartment that my younger sister and I had once used. If you did not know of the existence of this small facility you might not even notice it. The only thing to mark it is a large yellow sign that you can see from the nearby highway. They went there and while filling out the paperwork began talking to the people there. Now the thing she did not realize was that in the back of that facility are the offices of a very special group of people. My sister, being who she is, started talking to the people there about what was happening to me. As she soon found out the group of people in the back worked for an activist group called CCHR, Citizens Commission for Human Rights. This group works all over the United States to correct and stop psychiatric abuses. My sister met a man there who was also trying to stop electroshock in Texas with the Coalition for the Abolition of Electroshock in Texas (CAEST). They chatted for a while and he asked her to bring me for a video interview. I do not remember how she was able to get me dressed or get me to the office but indeed she did and that was my second step to recovery.

I arrived and I met all of the gentlemen that work there and they introduced themselves to me, though to be honest I could not remember their names three seconds after they said them. The one man, though, that made the biggest impact in my life was Dr. John Breeding. He often works with the other men there who make up most of the Texas CCHR group, he was a founding member of CAEST. John led me and my sister back to what looked like a conference room/library. He sat my sister and me at the table and explained what they would be doing. First John would introduce my sister and me and discuss why we were doing the video then he would ask us a few questions and have both of us explain what had happened to me and my family since being subjected to electroshock therapy. The video lasts for about 10 or 15 minutes and is posted on the above listed website and on www.youtube.com .

After that initial meeting John asked Kathy to see how many of my records from the psychiatric hospital she could obtain. My sister went to get the records, but they are by no means all of my records. Several weeks of my records were missing. In addition my sister paid nearly $300 to get copies of my own records. John had several people review my records to see if there were problems and if I had grounds for a suit. There were several things left out of the records and the report also stated that I was subjected to more electroshock in a six month period than was permitted in Texas. The problem with this type of suit is that in Texas you have a two year period from the incident to sue any medical personnel. Of course the doctors involved in psychiatry and electroshock know this and in addition they also know that by the time the patient had enough of their wits about them to bring a suit the time frame is past. This is one of the many reasons this practice has not been stopped. Most patients either never recover enough to sue the doctors involved or it is too late, as in my case. These same doctors also say that the patients are cured but that is an out and out lie. What happens is that the patient's brains are scrambled to the point that they cannot function normally. This makes most people very compliant and they accept anything the doctors say as truth. The families involved are just happy that their family member seems calmer. What happened to me was that I was indeed compliant but I also became more paranoid and as my feelings had no outlet I took them out on myself. I can't speak for others who have gone through electroshock but from what I have since read there are more people that had my experience than not. The review board report said I had justification for a suit but the time frame was past so all I could do was file a complaint which would be put in the doctor's files.

A few weeks later the end of shock folks had a protest outside of the hospital which subjected me to electroshock. John wanted me and my sister to come march and protest with them. My sister went but she could not get me to leave my room. I was just too anxious to be in a large group of people I did not know; however, that was not to be the end of my sister trying to get me out of my room. She conspired with John to get me to a rally and concert at which they were honoring electroshock victims that were speaking out. The event was The Fifth Annual Roky Erickson Psychedelic Ice Cream Social (see www.endofshock.com for a short video of the event). At this social they were honoring not only the famous rock

81

singer, who had himself been subjected to numerous electroshock treatments, but many others as well. They wanted to give me an honor as well and have me step up on the stage to speak. I do not remember all my sister had to do in order to get me there but I do seem to recall that she said she would kidnap me if she had to. In the end I finally dressed myself and went. It was a huge crowd at the original Threadgills restaurant in Austin, TX. I remember I was so overwhelmed by the huge crowd that I ended up pacing back and forth at the back of the crowd. Then they announced my name and asked me to come to the stage to get my award. I don't remember most of what I said but do remember speaking about true informed consent for electroshock. I then remember the band that was there started playing a song and I danced with them on the stage. That was the beginning of my voice being heard and it was a powerful thing indeed. I felt that no one understood what had happened to me and it was entirely my fault and here was a large group of people telling me that I was not alone and it was not my fault. From that point on I really began to examine what I had been told in regards to electroshock.

A couple of weeks later members of the Coalition spoke at the Austin City Council and they asked me to speak as well. When I was called to speak I stood and went to the microphone in the aisle. Inside I felt very small and that what I was doing would make no true difference. Taking a deep breath I began to speak. I had made notes so I would remember everything I wanted to say. The words are no longer in my memory but the feeling of empowerment that small act of defiance created in myself is still there and when I am feeling very small and as if I can't make a difference I remember that speech. Truly most of the people I spoke to that day do not even remember this woman and it did not change the minds of the city council in relation to electroshock, but it truly began a change in me. I stood up and spoke the truth about electroshock and what this awful abuse had done to me and to others in my situation. What awoke in me that day was my voice; no longer would I just accept what was told to me as truth. To be sure the change did not just happen overnight; it was and is truly a process, but the seed was planted that fateful day. I returned home and things went on as they had before, but my thoughts began to change even though I was not consciously aware of it yet.

A few weeks later I again started to cut myself, which resulted in my returning once again to the psychiatric hospital. I had not been back to the hospital since stopping electroshock about a year before. As it turns out this was to be the last time for me to return to Shoal Creek hospital as a patient. The only staff member I remembered was my social worker friend as he was the only person I really bonded with the entire time I was there. One thing that happened this time was a direct result of my finding and using my voice; when I signed myself into the hospital I refused to have my former psychiatrist, Dr. Lam assigned to me again. Then when I arrived on the floor they twice more tried to force me to see the same psychiatrist again and twice more I refused to see him. In fact I refused to sign myself in if they insisted that I see Lam again. This was truly the first time I had used my new found voice to express what I would accept and what I would not. It is especially important that even after I had signed in and was again told I would see my former psychiatrist that I twice more refused to be treated by him. Eventually they assigned me another psychiatrist. At the time I did not see this event as the life changing circumstance that it turned out to be. I had just climbed another rung of the ladder on my way to recovery.

When I saw this psychiatrist I told him how the drugs I was taking made me feel. I was having hallucinations as well as walking in my sleep. In addition I told him my memory was gone and I got lost every time I left my house. He looked at the list of 7 psychiatric drugs I was on and took me off of several and changed others still and reduced the dosage on several drugs as well. The result was that although I was still taking several psychiatric drugs the dosages were more reasonable and I was completely off of several of the drugs I was taking. From that point onward I really started finding my old self. I could think more clearly I could sleep more normally though I still had some insomnia. The hallucinations disappeared as did the sleep walking. By the time I left the hospital that time I felt truly human for the first time in about three years.

While in the hospital that week I did something else I had not done before. I refused to attend some of Shoal Creek hospital's "mandatory" meetings. I am convinced that most of that is to prevent the people from getting into trouble. I looked at those classes and meetings and flat out refused to go to many of them. One meeting was supposed to be for individuals to speak about problems and feelings they were having and then everyone could comment (supposedly positively) about the issue and offer insights. These meetings always turned into most individuals being petty and rude to each other. After attending one of these meetings I refused to go to another. They also had a class for recreational activities such as arts and crafts or music. I did not see the point of going and making a stupid craft. I was not there for arts and crafts. Don't get me wrong I love doing arts and crafts at home, but, I already know how to do this. How does it help me to go to a class like that? I was beginning to look for true help with the emotional problems and this place was not helping me with my quest. The only person there who had ever helped me with anything was my friend the social worker.

While there I began to consider changing another part of my life that was causing me great grief. I was grateful that my older sister asked me to live with her but our family dynamics were steadily going downhill. So I began to think about moving out on my own. There were several issues with this, one being the cost and another being me to think clearly enough to take care of myself while alone. I talked to my social worker friend about places that were for very low income people. He did a lot of research and gave me a lot of information to consider when I got home. It would be about another year before I was able to move out on my own but that helped plant another seed in my brain.

At the end of the week I returned home and although my situation did not immediately improve it did begin to change in subtle ways. My thinking began to slowly change as I was now able to at least begin to think for myself. I was thinking about moving out on my own and I was thinking about getting around the city on my own without my sister taking me everywhere. So I applied for housing and got put on the list and then I started going places on the city bus by myself.

I don't know how many people have ever tried to decipher a bus schedule and where to get on and off of the bus, but it is daunting for someone with all of their faculties intact much less someone with impaired reasoning abilities. The first place I remember going is to my primary care doctor's office. The good thing is it was a straight shot from my apartment to the office. First I had to walk about two blocks to the corner where there was a bus terminal. Then I had to get on the correct bus. I knew which bus I wanted to get on but what I did not know was that the same bus would leave that terminal and one would go west and one would go east. Lucky for me I had enough presence of mind to ask the driver if I was getting on the right bus. One thing I have learned since becoming a bus rider is that most bus drivers, at least in my town, are happy to help. He told me that I was getting on the bus going the wrong way; I wanted the east bound bus. I had to look for a bus that had the same number but the caption under the number would tell which way it was going. The next bus that came I checked again and I finally got on the right one. I climbed on the bus then I found a place to sit. This particular bus has seats up front for those individuals with physical disabilities so I was able to sit up front. I had not been on a city bus for more than 20 years and had never ridden a bus in Austin. This town has the most amazing mixture of people using city transit that you have ever seen. At first I did not know how to react. I was still having some panic in large groups and I definitely was nervous about doing this alone. The next hurdle was that I had to know which stop to get off at. I told the driver where I was going and he told me where to get off and reminded me when I got there. Not all bus drivers are this helpful but most are and they have saved me more than once. The ride to the stop was not long-about 15 minutes, but I sat in a corner trying to be small and inconspicuous. After I had gotten off at the right stop I had to remember which way the doctor's office was and walk there, which as it turned out was about half a mile. Walking several blocks is normally not a difficult thing for most people, but as I had not walked more than a block or two for a long time. I had a bad knee and arthritis and I was exhausted by the time I arrived. I checked myself in and had my checkup then came time for the return trip.

I had to walk all the way back to the corner and then I had to find the bus stop on the correct side of the street. This particular bus goes both ways on this street;

this is not true for all bus routes as I found out the hard way a few weeks later. I got to the bus stop and rode back home then walked the two blocks to my apartment. A trip like this may seem like a small thing to most people but to me it was a very big event. That was the first thing I had done alone since I had stopped driving a couple of years ago. I am glad that outing went so well or I may not have had the guts to try again.

I was so elated that I was able to go on an outing alone with no assistance that the next day I decided to try another outing on my own. I decided to go to visit my younger sister and her partner who live on the same bus route I had just ridden but in the opposite direction. The thing is I never told anyone where I was going I just left the house and got on the bus. Having ridden the bus once alone I thought I had everything figured out and so going to my sister's house would be no problem. I boarded the bus and I remember thinking this would be a short trip as my younger sister's home was only about 10 minutes away by car. I started talking to people on the bus and was not paying close attention to where I was going. As the bus traveled the route toward my sister's home I realized that since it was dark it was harder to tell where the bus was going and where I was in relation to my sister's home. At one point I asked a passenger where I should get off. I told her where my sister lived and she told me I should get off at the next bus stop. I thanked her and did just that. The neighborhood we had been passing through looked similar to my sisters but as I soon found out it was not the same. I got off of the bus and immediately realized that I had no idea where I was. It was dark and I had just gotten off of the last bus to come this way for the day. Now my brain finally computed what a fix I was in. I had told no one where I was going. I had gotten off the bus in an unfamiliar neighborhood and to top things off I had no phone and no way to contact my family to let them know where I was. I started walking down the street looking for anything familiar but only became more disoriented as I went. It was later than I had thought and I knew no one or really even saw anyone on this street. Finally I started down a nearby street hoping to find someone that would let me use their phone. I went up to several houses and knocked and either no one was home or they did not answer the door. I guessed that in this neighborhood it was not really safe to open the door to strangers at this time of day. Finally a nice man opened the door. It took several tries and help with translation from his daughter, as the man only spoke Spanish, but he finally let me use his cell while I was standing on his porch. When I got my younger sister on the phone of course the first thing she asked was where I was. I had absolutely no idea where I was. I thought I was near a fire station and school that we knew in her area and said so but did not even have enough cognitive processes to find out what street corner I was on. I asked the man who loaned me the phone and after much back and forth he finally understood what I was asking and told me the name of the street. I told my sister I would wait on the corner for her which I did after thanking the gentleman who helped me. The unfortunate part was that I was not near the school and fire station that I thought I was. My sister and her partner immediately went to the fire station I thought I was at to get me and could not find me. They drove around that neighborhood for some time and never found the street name I told them. The two of them were by now frantic and very angry with me, so went back to the fire station and pounded on the door for several minutes until someone answered the door. They described me and asked if I had been there; of course the fire men had never seen me. They got the firemen to call the police and then started to look for me again. My sister's partner remembered another school and fire house in a nearby area and started toward that station.

By this time I had been waiting on the corner for some time and had really become anxious about staying there alone. My mind conjured up all kinds of things from crack dealers to who knows what to scare myself. I became so anxious that I started walking down the road I was on instead of staying put and waiting on my family. As I walked I saw a pile of large things left out for the trash collectors. My mind immediately flew off in another direction as I spotted something in the trash pile that I thought I would like to take. Being that I could not keep my mind on one thought for more than a millisecond I picked up the object and started walking down the road with it. I don't even remember what it was that I picked up from the trash except that it had legs on it and was obviously light enough for me to carry.

It never occurred to me that I should not have left the corner where I said I would be. I just walked on oblivious to the world. I walked to a dead end and it was a school. I briefly considered trying to cross the campus but it was fenced off and so I was forced to turn around and start walking back the way I had come. It was not long after that my sister and her partner found me wandering back down this dead end street with the piece of furniture in my hand. They turned around and came back to me and only when they stopped the car did I realize it was my sister. She opened the door and yelled at me to get in. I at first tried to get in the car with the object I was holding only to be told that I had to leave it. I did not want to do this but they eventually convinced me to leave it. As I got in the car I realized my sister and her partner were not only frantic but that they were angry with me as well. Now as I write this I understand their fear and anger at me but to be truthful at the time I did not understand their anger. I am sure that my response infuriated them all the more. To this day I do not think they understood, as most people would not, that I had no clue as to why they were so angry with me. I know that sounds stupid but my brain was barely functioning and to look at me you would not know that. I don't know for sure but I think that is why it is so hard for people to understand what is happening in the mind of someone that screwed up on drugs and electroshock. It is not visible to the naked eye and a lot of the time I could carry on a sensible conversation and even carry out familiar tasks. Then my brain would go haywire and I would do something so completely nonsensical and stupid that most people, including most doctors, would assume I was behaving in those ways just to get attention. This is unfortunately the way that biopsychiatry works. Then of course the psychiatrists, who should and do know better, just add more labels and drugs and electroshock. After that incident my sister and her partner got me a cell phone so that I could call anyone I needed any time. They of course had to program the phone numbers into the phone and teach me to use it and carry it with me no matter where I went.

One of the things I had to agree to while in the hospital the last time was to engage a private therapist and see this therapist each week. So shortly after the above incident I was going to a documentary about Roky Erickson with friends from CCHR, including John whom I knew was a therapist and so I asked him if he knew of someone who could provide me with therapy each week. He agreed to do this for me and we have worked together for more than four years now. To tell you the truth I did not know what to expect. I was nervous about going as I had gone to one therapist for a short time while seeing my first psychiatrist and I quit because I could not afford her and we did not fit. Her style was much more the mainstream that went along with the accepted norms of psychiatry which instead of helping me only caused further hurt to me. My sister brought me each week to sessions with John. I can't remember all we talked about but we clicked which I can tell you is the most important thing in therapy. I felt safe with him as I had not felt safe with anyone in my life since becoming involved with psychiatry. As the weeks passed I began to open up about what was really hurting me. I could not begin to tell you what that was at the beginning of therapy, mostly because I still have little memory of that time. Whatever it was we talked about I began to slowly come out of my shell and began to heal myself.

Shortly thereafter one night, I began to have severe chest pains and had a hard time breathing. I called my sister in and told her what was happening and she immediately called 911. I spent two nights in the hospital and had tests on my heart but in the end they decided that the problem was a reaction to a psychiatric drug I had been placed on called Geodon. This drug not only caused irregularities in my heartbeat, but was also causing me to urinate on myself when asleep. Both are well-known side effects of this particular drug. They took me off of Geodon and put me back on Zoloft and sent me home. What this did for me was begin to wake me up to the fact that all of these drugs that were so routinely used all had serious effects and reactions that I knew nothing about. So when I went back to therapy with John we began to talk about drugs and their effects and my reactions to them and how they really work in your body.

The next hurdle was to find a psychiatrist that would accept someone only with Medicare and no secondary insurance. Up until that time I had no idea that private practice psychiatrists do not accept individuals on Medicare only. This should be a clue that their main focus is not the patient. However, I finally found a newly practicing psychiatrist who was willing to accept a Medicare only client. As I began to see him I was still very messed up on many psychiatric drugs. He agreed to begin weaning me off of some of the drugs. This I can tell you is a very rare thing indeed.

I was slowly but steadily improving because I was getting off of the drugs that had nearly killed me and I was finally starting to deal with the things that had led to my breakdown in the first place. Then a few short weeks later I had just returned home with my younger sister's partner when I picked up the phone. The following is the short conversation I had. "Is this the daughter of John Scogin?" "Yes, I am Evelyn Scogin one of his daughter's." "This is the nurse from Valley View nursing home and I am sorry to inform you that your father has just died". "You have got to be kidding." "No ma'am I would not kid about a thing like that." "We will be there shortly." For any person this would have been a life-changing event; as for me the death of my father brought up lots of feelings I had yet to process or deal with and as a result I again went into an emotional crisis which resulted in me feeling suicidal. The unique thing about this crisis was that after talking to John on the phone he suggested that he see me every day at my home for the next couple of weeks instead of me again returning to the hospital. I agreed and for the next few weeks we worked very closely with the feelings of hopelessness and helplessness I was feeling and I was able to begin to see where these feelings originated from. Feelings of guilt and grief related to my relationship with my father were some of the issues I was dealing with. I do not wish to give the idea that by dealing with these issues once they went away. I continue to battle some of these same feelings today, but as I understand where some of these feelings originated, I was able to make space for feelings of worth and love.

As I moved forward in my recovery, relationships between myself and my nephews and sister, whom I lived with suffered. My nephews began to argue more and had not only screaming matches but a few fist fights as well. At one point one of my nephews became so angry that he threatened me and then pushed his mother into a corner and tried to hit her. I was still under the influence of many drugs so my thinking was still not very clear, but I ran outside with my cell phone and called the police. However, I was so upset that I could not tell the police my address or even the name of my apartment or my phone number. The police had to keep me on the phone until they could trace the call and find where I was and send help. By the time they arrived the argument was over but they asked my nephew to go to a friend's home for a couple of days and calm down. I understand that my behavior, on top of the fact that both of my nephews were living and sleeping in a small living room lead to their feelings of resentment and they had nowhere to go any more than I did. The next day an agent from Adult Protective Services showed up at the apartment because I was considered disabled and there was concern that I was being abused or taken advantage of. Eventually both of my nephews found other places to live with friends. One nephew now lives in north Texas with his now fiancé and the other nephew lives across town with his fiancé. They both seem to be happy with how their lives are developing. While I don't know if they understand where my behavior and theirs originated, at least they are glad that I am continuing to recover and relearn how to take care of myself.

That same December I decided to have a major surgery that I had needed for some time. I had been on Medicare for about a year and when they renewed it they sent me a notice that appeared as if I not only qualified for Medicare but for Medicaid as well. To be sure this was true I called Medicare and spoke to a person who told me that was indeed true but until I got a permanent card I was to go to the local Health and

Human Services offices and get a temporary card each month. Since I now had Medicare and Medicaid I could afford to go to an orthopedic surgeon to get help with my knees, which had been very painful for some years.

The surgeon told me that both knees were so bad that there was bone on bone contact and they needed to be replaced. I decided to start with my right knee which was somewhat worse than the left and that December I had the surgery. The surgery went well and I was recovering as predicted but for a couple of months I had to take some pretty strong pain killers. Pain killers act in many of the same ways as do psychotropic drugs. So I had to go through the process of withdrawal from the effects of these drugs as well as the other drugs I was trying to get off of. There were several months of inability to sleep as well as irritability and nervousness and crying jags. The process of withdrawal is not an easy process for anyone, which is why to this day one thing I do before I take a new drug or treatment recommended by any doctor is my own research first. At the end of my three months of physical therapy I was finally beginning to think for myself and began writing about my experiences in small ways.

Then in February of that year my relationship with the family members that I was living with came to a head and we had another argument. At this point I had gotten, for the moment, the student loan people to stop taking $150 out of my disability check and thus had enough money to finally move out on my own. My sister's partner called me up and said you have enough money, let's go look for an apartment for you. So I did, on March 15th 1998. That day will stay in my mind forever. After picking the apartment out I slept with a copy of the floor plan under my pillow and dreamt of my own place every night.

As I had lived with my sister for a couple of years I no longer had many of the things I needed to live alone. I had my bedroom furniture but not living room furniture or dishes and pans and such for the kitchen. I also had to engage a mover and turn on electricity and put a down payment on my apartment as well as sign the contract. I was excited to finally be able to do these things almost by myself. My younger sister still had to sign my checks and give me money for anything I needed. In fact, although my sister was helping and I love her for it, I did not go shopping for pots and pans and dishes and things for myself as she and her partner did that for me, mostly because it was just simpler for her to do that rather than to come and get me and us do it together. I did call and set up the mover myself and a very good friend put the move on her credit card and let me pay her back over several months.

Descent

Because We Can

Do you know what I am Tired of?
The "Because we can" syndrome
Not many companies or people are brazen enough to
actually say that
but it is implied in every action of the people and
companies with the money.
They do it so much they know that most people will just
give up and go away.

I recently rented an apartment with my sister. Before I
signed the lease I was told
"Oh yes we will provide any accommodation you need.
You want a ramp for your wheel chair.

Yes we can do that. You need bathroom
accommodations. We can do that too."
I signed the lease.
"But wait you have to pay for any changes yourself.
And oh by the way when you leave you have to take all
of the changes out.
Why? Because then we would be required to make
those changes for anyone."

I recently received a settlement offer from a well-known
drug company.
I can't tell you the details because that too is part of the
settlement.
Oh, and by the way the settlement is not because our
drug did any harm
But just because paying you off is easier than fighting
the suit.

"It does not matter that the people who took your drug
are harmed for the rest of their lives."

We have the money and therefore the power
And "because we can" we will continue to sell our drug
and hurt people.
Because we have the money and power.
We have better public relations so the public will believe
what we tell them.

The psychiatrists who put me on all of the drugs and
electroshock
Have been given their status power and money
Because they sell the products of the drug companies
And the companies who make and sell the electroshock
machines.
Because they have the power and money
"Because they can" label people and have the better
public relations
no one wants to listen to the truth.

"Because they can" is no longer good enough.
Because they have convinced the world that they know
what is best is no longer acceptable to me.
I may not change the minds of all or even most who
listen to me,
but I finally heard the truth of what "they" are doing.
If one person reading this hears the truth
then they convince one other person
eventually the world will know what "they" are doing.
I no longer accept that "because they" have the money
and power and "can"
I have no power.
To have the courage to speak the truth and continuing
to speak the truth nullifies the truth that
"Because they can I can't"

Descent

Chapter 6

Dissent

The best slave

does not need to be beaten

She beats herself

Erica Jong, "Alcestis on the Poetry Circuit" (1)

It was a giant step forward for me to move into a place on my own even if I still had to have help from family for transportation and money management. I could do as it pleases me in my own home and set up my apartment the way I wanted. When I looked at apartments, one of the things I made sure I told the leasing office was that I needed my apartment to be on the ground floor as I was looking into getting a motorized wheel chair. Then came the day of the big move and I had to go to the apartment office to sign the contract and pick-up the keys to my apartment which I had yet to see. My older sister stayed at her apartment and directed the movers on what to bring so I could get the keys and meet them at my apartment. When I arrived at the office the apartment was not ready and they had neglected to let me know. The movers had to wait around for a couple of hours while the maintenance men finished installing new carpet. So you can imagine my surprise when I arrived at my apartment to find there was a small set of stairs leading to it. I found out the hard way that all of the apartments were built like modular or mobile homes and then brought to the site and constructed one on top of the other; therefore the foundation was like a mobile home and all of the apartments had stairs in front of them. First of all this caused the move to cost more as well as the fact that I could not bring a wheel chair into the apartment. For that moment I was stuck and could do nothing about it except move into the apartment as it was. This issue would crop up many times later, however.

After moving into my apartment I again began to teach myself to ride the city bus system. Since getting lost several months before my family was afraid to let me out of their sight and to be honest I was just a little nervous about getting lost as well. However, I decided that I needed to learn to move about on my own again. I would not be limited to only going places when my family had time or wanted to take me there. Thus I began exploring using several city services for the disabled and those with low income. I called the bus company and asked about services for disabled as I remembered that my disabled students rode the bus for free. It turns out at that time, though it has recently changed, that indeed with a special bus pass I could ride the bus anywhere for free. They sent me the paperwork for my doctor to fill out which he did and my sister took me downtown to get my pass and my first city bus schedule. I had never been a bus rider in Austin except for a couple of times with students just in the downtown area so I really did not know how the system worked. I now could give classes to anyone trying to learn to ride this city bus system and believe me it is often a very confusing system indeed. There were many times I got on the wrong bus and found myself in the wrong part of the city. Eventually I developed a system that worked for me. At the time I did not have cable or internet services so I could not access the system that way, a true advantage which I do have now. When I wanted to go somewhere on the bus I found the address and looked it up on the bus schedule and tried to find the closest street to the address listed. This is difficult because not all of the stops are listed on the schedule even when looked up on the internet. I would find where I wanted to go and the time I needed to catch each bus and write all of the directions on a piece of paper. Then when I got on the first bus I would ask the bus driver if he knew where the stop was and often he did, but there have been times when the driver would give me the wrong stop and I had to end up walking a lot farther than needed or the nearest stop was a mile or more away from my destination. The walking between stops and to my final destination quickly became a hindrance to my moving about due to my physical pain. Often I would just not go places I wanted because I had to walk too far or it would take several bus changes and several hours to get there. In fact I knew that would quickly become an issue when I moved out on my own as I had no car and my family was busy with their own lives.

As I wanted to become more independent and function without aid of my family I started looking into getting a motorized wheelchair. When my father died he had a wheelchair, but as it had sat in my younger sister's garage for about a year the batteries were dead so I called a wheelchair company to come and fix it. Would Medicare pay for the cost? Because the chair was bought with my father's Medicare, I unfortunately discovered that the system would not pay for fixing that chair even though it was still a very nice chair. The system instead would only pay for a brand new chair for me if I could go through the whole process of getting a doctor to write a prescription for one for me and then send it to the company. The other issue is that the chair would only be approved by my insurance if it was for use mainly inside my apartment. Well I really needed to use the wheelchair to travel outside my apartment to get to places on the bus, etc. The company I was working with then sent a therapist out to measure me for the chair, which was ordered and delivered in about three weeks. This company billed Medicare for their part but never charged me for the remaining cost.

While all of this was going on I began a monumental struggle with my apartment complex to get my apartment adapted for wheelchair use. As I was a special education teacher for almost 8 years, not to mention that I had worked with multiply handicapped people for about 20 years, you would think I would know how to get services I needed. The truth is until I tried to get services for myself I had no idea what was involved, as I am sure most people do not until they need them and then have no one to guide them. I naively thought that all I would need to do was call the apartment complex and explain what my problem was and like magic they would do as I asked; boy was I wrong. The manager was surprised that I even brought the subject up as she said she knew nothing about my needs. I explained that I had told the leasing agent my needs before moving into my apartment. At any rate what I needed at that point in time was to have a ramp so that I could get a wheelchair in and out of my apartment and to the various bus stops that were located nearby. The apartment said they would get back to me in a few days. In the meantime I saw them come and look at how a ramp could be installed. I could see that from that particular apartment it would be quite a task to install a ramp as they also had to consider that a ramp could only have a specific incline and had to thus extend the length quite some distance from my apartment. Furthermore, on the landing in front of my apartment there was a staircase and my door would have to have a small ramp. Several days later I did get a call from them that said they had a person moving at the beginning of the next month that was in a handicap accessible apartment and would I consider moving if they had a mover come at no charge. This was just fine with me and so on the first of July I moved into the assessable apartment. There was a ramp out front and the bathroom was already wheelchair assessable with bars and a special raised toilet. All of the interior doorways were wider so a wheelchair would fit through. I was satisfied until the time came for me to be fitted for my wheelchair and the therapist measuring me pointed out that the ramp in front needed to be fixed as part of it was wooden deck and part was poured cement and where the two met the wooden deck dropped down about 2 inches; there was also a lip of about the same depth at the front door. About the same time I also noticed there was no handicapped parking space so my sister could come and pick me up. Two other things became clear when I walked the property; one was that the mail room was not accessible by wheelchair and all of the doors at the office and my apartment were of the regular knob turning type. All of these things needed to be changed by the time my wheelchair arrived. I again called the manager to discuss these issues at which point she began stalling about completing these tasks. Finally in mid-March of 2009 my chair arrived but none of the repairs had been completed. In addition a further problem had cropped up in the apartment I had relocated to, a problem that had nothing to do with accessibility rules but everything to do with my daily life.

The water in my apartment took at least 20 minutes to get hot and that with all of the hot taps running at full speed as my water pressure was also low. Finally one day I called the manager and told her I had had enough of the stalling and that she would fix these items as they were her responsibility. She finally admitted to me that she had no intention of fixing anything without me paying for it myself. I had never run across someone so opposed to doing what was clearly not only the right thing but the apartment's responsibility so I called the management company to complain and got pretty much the same story.

I had no money to fix any of these issues and they were clearly the responsibility of the management but I did not know how to force the issue. This would in the past have probably been the point at which I would have given up as pushing for things for myself was something I was not comfortable doing. I would have fought tooth and nail to get services for any of the individuals I taught or worked with in the past but for myself I would just give up. Not this time, I had finally had enough of getting run over and just accepting it and then somehow blaming myself for what was happening to me. I might not win but I would not go down without a fight. I was beginning to see that I was not at fault for everything that happened to me and I had a voice and a right to be heard and not just dismissed out of hand because I was poor and had as they saw it few choices left to me. I got on the phone and called a number that became my friend in need and if there was any one resource that was the place to go to start searching for answers it was this. I picked up the phone and called 311. I don't know if all states have this service but they have pointed me to resources that I had no idea how to connect with in Texas and (are managed by the United Way) 311 has resources for local city, county, and state services and I told them what my problem was and they told me who to talk to.

The first number I called did not have the answers I needed but they lead me to another resource who led me to another resource, etc. until I had the answers and the help I needed. I finally talked to a woman who was in charge of seeing that local and state agencies followed and applied all of the state and federal ADA (Americans with Disabilities Act) rules. She explained to me that any apartment has to pay for anything that will get me from the parking lot to the interior of my apartment as well as any areas that are for general public use that is if they were built after 1991 or are receiving tax or other incentives. When you get to the interior of the apartment they do not have to pay for materials but have to make all requested changes to make the apartment usable to the tenant and they can further request the tenant pay to have those changes reversed when they leave. However, most apartments will make those reasonable changes the tenant requires because this makes the apartment more easily rented even though they cannot charge more for said apartment. She then gave me the number for the local tenant's council which I never knew existed. I called and got in touch with the person who oversees the water and a second person who oversees compliance with ADA rules. This process took a couple of weeks to complete but the information I gained was invaluable.

The following week first the person who oversees the water came to test my hot water and he said that since he tested the temperature and in 3 or 4 minutes it did not get hot he considered there to be no hot water. A letter was then sent to the office management but a copy was sent to me as well. In the letter he said that if the water issue was not fixed, or at least trying to be repaired within 7 days, he would begin citing them for a health violation for which they would have to pay a fine. They ignored this letter and I called this officer back who came back and again tested the water then went to the office and cited them for a health violation. The next morning the head of the management company was at my door saying I should have called her before things had gotten this far and they would fix the problem ASAP. They checked the boiler and something was broken there that was preventing my water from heating properly. They changed this part and for several weeks the problem was solved before cropping up again.

The same week that the water officer came the woman that oversaw ADA compliance came to my apartment and I explained the situation and the things that I needed changing so I could use my wheelchair. She measured all the places I needed ramps or needed them fixed and noted all the changes that needed to be made to the property. She wrote a letter, which I again received a copy detailing what changes needed to be made and why. The letter further stated that if these changes were not begun immediately then tenant's council and I would have no choice but to sue them.

The manager was furious and called telling me that I would have to pay for part of the cost of repairs, etc. These tactics continued until I gave them the name of the lawyer I talked to about these issues and the woman from the tenant's council sent a second letter. The day after receiving this second letter there was someone there to fix the ramp leading from the parking lot to the porch in front of my home. However, the manager still would not have my parking space marked and painted until one day I blew a gasket and called her up and said, "I don't care who I have to call to have my space marked off by the end of the day; if it is the mayor or the newspapers or the president I will do it." By the time I arrived home several hours later the sign had been placed and the spaces marked off so not only could my sister park but I would have space to enter the car as well. I do not ever recall talking to another human being so harshly but I meant every single word I said and it felt good to finally use my voice and not be ignored. Finally at least one small victory for Evelyn!

The very next week the manager and all but one of the leasing agents had been replaced by the management company. When I asked why I was only told they were sent to a different property. I personally think they were moved primarily to delay the repairs that still needed to be made to the property for me. I started talking to the new manager about what I had requested and she knew nothing about what had been going on. I had to get her to go through my file and find all of the letters and complaints I had made. She of course had to speak with the management company about these continued issues. I lost my temper as I had already been through this with the other manager and still I was getting stonewalled. I finally called the woman from the tenant's council who had come out and sent the original letter. A second letter was sent saying if these repairs were not taken care of in short order we would have no choice but to sue them. The manager called me and started talking to me about what kinds of ramps we could get for my front door and for the mail room. The alleged big issue was that they were told that these ramps would get in the way of people trying to pass my door or use the mailroom and my door and pose a tripping hazard; this could not have been farther from the truth. The management company was just trying to find ways not to comply with these reasonable and required requests. I still do not know why they were being so obstinate. They were not very expensive repairs for the apartment to make. The outlay of expenses for a suit would undoubtedly be much more costly. I don't know what the manager said to the company to convince them, but she did some internet research and ordered rubber ramps for my door and the mail room, both of which probably cost them less than $500 dollars. It was a few weeks before they arrived but we all celebrated when they were installed with special cement. I was now able to go everywhere on the property and to and from the bus stop without impediments and without damage to my chair. Score another one for the good guys.

The next challenge was actually maneuvering in a wheelchair in the real world. First time I decided to ride the bus, which I had already checked out and knew all of the city buses are wheelchair accessible, I determined I would just go down the street to the grocery store. I got in my chair, which I was still learning how to control, and got to the front door which I had to open, then move out of the way go through the door, then turn and try to close it. I found out something anyone who has used a wheelchair knows and it is that you can't close the door while sitting in the chair. I ended up having to get out of the door to close it. I am lucky enough to use the chair for distance travel so I could actually perform this maneuver while others are not so lucky. Eventually I would attach old man's ties to the levers of the inside and outside of the door so I could close it without getting out of the chair again. Now that my apartment was secure and I know where to get on and off the bus, I took my chair and rolled to the bus stop. On the way other new obstacles presented themselves which I had never noticed before. Funny how a change in the way you see the world changes the obstacles placed in front of you. The ends of all of the sidewalks in front of my apartment where they meet the curbs were not even. Due to the fact that there had been a drought the last couple of years the sidewalks and curbs did not match and are just like my front door without a ramp. If I work my way over them it would eventually tear up my chair. I would worry about that as soon as I got home. I got to the bus stop and discovered there was protocol for loading a wheelchair on the bus; again I had not paid any attention to this prior to my accessing the bus in my chair. The bus driver is supposed to make the other passengers wait to get onto the bus until the wheelchair is loaded and locked into place. Sometimes the passengers do not wait and the bus driver can't or doesn't make them follow the rules. There have been times when the bus is so full that several passengers have to get off of the bus and wait while the person in the chair is loaded then they can get back on and stand in the aisle because my chair unfortunately takes up 3 to 5 seats depending on the type of bus. The driver lowered the ramp and I pulled on, then immediately had problems maneuvering into place and scanning my card. It took me several tries as I had never had to maneuver in such a small space before. I was embarrassed as I could see that the passengers and driver were aggravated at having to wait on me. I got on the bus and the driver hooked my chair up so it would not move or turn over. Then it drove the three blocks to the next bus stop at which point I had to get off. I needed to let the driver know I was getting off here. Most people just pull the cord overhead, a thing I could not do, so instead I just shouted up to the driver I was getting off here. He was trying to help as he could see that this was my first time to use the wheelchair access and told me there was a special button next to me that I should push to alert him. By this time I was red in the face at having put out so many people and then when I tried to maneuver off of the bus I got my chair stuck and accidentally pulled one of the brake levers into the off position on my chair. A motorized chair has brakes on each side of the chair that are turned off when a lever is pulled at the bottom of the chair next to the wheel and when one or both of these levers are tripped the motor will not run and an alarm goes off. Now I was stuck and could not move my chair; in fact although I knew about the brakes I did not know how to get the chair unstuck. I finally stood up and the bus driver literally picked the back end up until I could push the lever back into place and thus roll down the ramp. I was mortified and I had not even made it to the store yet.

I had yet to drive my chair through the parking lot to the door of the store without getting run over by a car.

Descent

All of these things were new experiences. As a special education teacher I thought I knew what my student's obstacles were; boy was I misinformed. I got into the store and to shop I had to balance a carry basket on the foot plate between my feet. Then of course I had to move through the aisles of the store. First of all the aisles are not really that big so there is no room to pass people who are in front of you, and if you are in a chair they just simply do not see you. I would have to wait patiently behind someone with a basket in front of me until they moved and then half of the time someone waiting behind me for me to move would simply dart in front of me as if I was not there. The next challenge was that most of the things I wanted on a shelf were out of reach and I either had to put the basket on the floor, that is if my lap was not full, or ask someone passing by if they would grab something for me. Happily, all of the times I have had to ask someone for help they have never refused to aid me. I think everyone should try shopping one day from a wheelchair and you will quickly see what the challenges and obstacles are. I think if we walk at least one day in the shoes of another and see what their challenges are then we would all be kinder to each other and we would not have so many troubles in the world. I dare anyone who reads this book to try shopping just once in one of those motorized wheelchairs provided at a store and see what I mean. Fortunately, the rest of my trip to the store was uneventful and I eventually became competent in moving around the world in my wheelchair, but not before I learned what it was to truly have barrier after barrier placed in my path. If nothing else this taught me that most of the time the world does not intentionally place barriers in your way; it is mostly due to not seeing things from the view of the other person. The flip side of this is that although you can educate people about these barriers, getting them to change things that effect their pocketbook, even when it is slight and it is the right

112

thing to do, will stop progress in its tracks almost every time. The key is to find the people that can support you through this process and keep speaking out and find a way to become a thorn in the side of the ones with the pocketbook.

Along with the many obstacles placed in my way at the same time there were also many taken out of my path by the acquisition of my motorized chair. I now felt like I was a real person again as I could get on the bus and travel any place the bus would take me without asking someone to take time out of their schedule to take me where I wanted to go. If you have ever had to depend on others for travel and have no other means to get around you might get a sense of what this meant to me. I quickly learned how to travel the bus system and when I gained a little more confidence I met lots of people on the bus who were happy to have a conversation about almost anything. In fact in Austin I would venture to say we have a large group of nonconformists and characters, if you take the time to talk to us, you will find us more alike than different and that we want the same things that all people want. I even found a way to go to my weekly therapy appointments on the city bus, although it did take about an hour on the bus and then I had to drive about a mile in my chair through the local neighborhoods to get there, but it meant everything to me.

After I began to see that everything was not my fault and I began improving my self-esteem then when these and other barriers were placed in my way I was for the most part eventually able to fight for my rights. That is not to say that I thought it was easy then or now, especially when you continually do not find the justice for all spoken of in the constitution. I sometimes stop and have a session of yelling and crying and hitting pillows because as much as we would like to believe it the world is not fair. However, now I have enough confidence in myself that I can dust myself off and start again fighting for that same justice for all; what a great county that at least we have the right to fight for justice.

While I was fighting for my rights I was also healing physically and emotionally and along the way new goals were formed. At the suggestion of John, my therapist, I began trying to write my story. It took a while to even get it started for many reasons. I have been working through my issues while writing many things have resolved for me and I have begun to reclaim the ability to use words. After electroshock therapy I lost the ability to recall many words easily and the ability to spell many words, not to mention many other effects which I will address later in this book, In November of 2008 John and I began discussing my return to work, and in December of that same year I took my last psychotropic drug. Ending psychiatric drug use had huge ramifications in my life, and has informed all subsequent decisions made in my life.

Today
Part II

Today with conscious thought
And all the free will I own
I have carefully chosen
What becomes one with
My body mind and spirit

Since clearing my mind
Of mind altering drugs and treatment
I have now reclaimed much of my former self
This was not a journey made alone,
But with the help and support of many dear friends and
family

I am now recovering
I live independently again
I can now drive a car
I have applied and interviewed for work
I still have little memory of my decline.
I still become lost at times,
But now have an action plan in place
So I can reorient myself quickly
My short term memory is much less short
I am now making new friends
I have healed many past hurts with my family
I am not the person I was before,
And that I think is in some ways a good thing
I have found myself again

Today I remember the struggles of my recent past,
And vow to never again just accept that the course of treatment
Prescribed for me is the truth I should follow
I will listen to what they have to say
Then I will research plans of treatment
And all of their ramifications
Then and only then
Will "I" choose the appropriate course of action

Today I choose to stand up and shout to anyone
Within the sound of my voice
To the state and federal government
And all of the powers that be
These hurtful outdated practices must stop
Especially ECT therapy!!!

This is my body mind and spirit
I gave it to the psychiatric community when I needed help
I took it back
My body mind and spirit are a non-negotiable demand

Chapter 7

Reclaiming Self

Hope begins in the dark, the stubborn hope that if you just show up and try to do the right thing, the dawn will come. You wait and watch and work: you don't give up.

Anne Lamott (1954-), Introduction to Bird by Bird: Some Instructions on Writing and Life, 1995(1)

In November I began to search for a job. I knew that in the fall, searching for a public school teaching job with my last position being a special education teacher, would be next to impossible. I started my search for positions as a case manager or QMRP (Qualified Mental Retardation Professional) at local state agencies. I was amazed that I got two interviews in a row and became excited because I thought I would have a job in short order. After all I had never before had a problem finding work. My skills in working with multi-handicapped are well documented and I have had twenty years experience. Well I did not get those jobs and when I began applying for teaching positions the next March I did not even get interviews. I know part of my problem was that I depended on the city bus system for transportation and therefore could only apply for positions within the city. Still and all I thought my skills, education, experience and good references would be enough.

They of course were not and so at the suggestion of my younger sister, I went to the local Department of Assistive and Rehabilitation Services. In order for them to assist me in any way I had to first fill out all kinds of paperwork and wait until they received confirmation of my disabilities from my doctors. There are many fine people who work for this agency. Unfortunately I had the bad luck of getting a counselor who was incompetent or lazy or both. She did not help me in any way with employment. Not only was she incompetent and lazy, she was condescending as well. I know these counselors are used to working with people with more limited intellectual abilities than mine but there was really no excuse for not receiving any help in the more than two years I was a client of the agency. I could now go back and ask for a different counselor and I am considering that but have not made a decision yet.

Now this is where things get really interesting. I called the Social Security department before I started to search for a job to find out the options for someone, like me, who is on SSDI (Social Security Disability Insurance) to find out what would happen if I did return to work. Well I can tell you the rules are so complicated that even the Social Security Administration screws it up all of the time. In fact it was only recently I found out the actual laws concerning this area. But, let me begin with the story I was given at the time I began my search. I called SSA and was told they had a program called return to work for those on disability, because getting your funds back after you have lost them when returning to work is almost impossible; therefore most people in the past did not even try to return to work. The issue for me and most people on SSDI is that even with additional help such as food stamps, housing, and Medicare/Medicaid; you do not have enough money to live on. Since I was a teacher I made more money than most people and I was able to receive $1000 a month; however, this put me in the bracket that I did not qualify for any help except for Medicare. This barely covered my rent and utilities and I had to depend on food banks for food and family for other help such as paying for doctors, Medicare only covers up to 80% of the medical bills. Not to mention I had student loans of originally 18,000 dollars from when I got my degree, a loan which due entirely to interest and late fees is now more than 45,000. When I talked to that first person at the Social Security Administration about the return to work program she described the following program. As long as I was actively searching for a job they would not have me go through the re-certification process that everyone goes through every two to five years in order to continue receiving disability. In addition I was told that I could work for a period of nine months consecutively and earn as much as I wished and not only keep my Medicare but continue getting my monthly disability check as well or I could work for a period of three consecutive years part time with the same rules applying. This was put in law to protect those trying to return to work, because as I soon discovered not only was it hard to get a job when you have been on disability, but it becomes equally as difficult to keep one.

During the period from November of 2008 to June of 2009 I must have applied for several hundred jobs with many different agencies working with special needs individuals and had maybe 5 or 6 interviews, but did not get one job offer. In fact to this day I still have only one interview for a teaching position. I asked each of the places that interviewed me what I could do to improve my chances to get a teaching position. For instance was it the way I answered questions or my experience, etc. and every one of them swore I was a very good candidate but someone with more experience got the job. I know this to be an untrue statement as I know not many people have as much and as varied experience in this field. I began working with special needs individuals in 1985 as a direct care provider then called a house parent. We provided care and supervision for 19 women with sometimes severe behavior issues in their dorm or home. This was my first real job and I was surprised that I was good at it; despite the stresses that went along with the job I actually enjoyed it. I worked for this "school" for almost ten years. During this same time period I also became fluent in American Sign Language and worked for the local school district in various classrooms as a sign language interpreter/classroom aide. After working in the classroom for a while I decided that I wanted to return to college and get a degree in Special Education, which I did while still working full time as a direct care aide. I graduated from Texas Woman's University in 1997 at the age of 40. At this point I began my career as a special education teacher and continued working as a teacher until I was forced to retire after becoming involved with psychiatry. Because of my experience and work history I could not understand why I was not getting interviews or being offered a job.

Finally in June of 2009 I received my first job offer from the state school in Austin working as a case manager. Basically I was to ensure that all of the programs for the individuals living on the unit I was working were in order and being followed. In addition I would fill out monthly reports and make sure everything was filed properly. I knew I could do this job and so I accepted and began orientation two weeks later.

In preparation for starting the orientation process I mapped out the route I would take to get to work on the bus. I needed to make sure I was leaving and arriving on time. So the Friday before I set my alarm clock just as if I were going to work on the bus in my wheelchair. I had to get up at 4:30am in order to get ready and be at the bus stop before 6:00. I had to change buses twice to get to work and I am glad I had the dry run because the first stop I was told to go to was the wrong one and so I missed the first connecting bus and had to take a second one. The real fun began when I arrived at my destination. The actual bus stop is directly across from the facility but it is a main thorough fare that I had to then cross in my wheelchair; although there was a curb cut there was no cross walk or light of any kind to stop traffic so one could safely cross. I could not believe that this facility that had been there since the 1950's and used this stop with their individuals had no safe place to cross. The campus itself has many buildings; some are clearly marked, others just have numbers so it took me several tries and about twenty minutes to find the building. I was amazed when I had come for interviews that a lot of those buildings are not handicap compliant. Most can be entered on the ground floor but almost none of them have elevators to the upper floors, so when I arrived I had to park my chair in the break room and negotiate the stairs to the classroom. While uncomfortable for me, this is not impossible. The problem came when the teachers found out I used a wheelchair to get to work every day. Yes, I can walk and move around indoors but walking from bus stop to my destination is a very long way and very uncomfortable for me. I told them that I could pass their classes and I did not lie but the wheelchair became my first obstacle. I really did not understand as I had yet to see any person on that campus go from one building to another without using their car. I explained that my wheelchair was my car. They looked at me askance and I could tell that they were not convinced but they let me stay in class. As I say this was just the first obstacle they put in my path. After accepting this position I was told that because this facility could not keep direct care staff when they were shorthanded I had to fill in in that capacity. That was okay with me as I had done that for many years.

The second complication arose when I was told as part of my orientation process that I had to be restrained by others and placed in a strait jacket. This little bomb was just dropped on us casually during class as if it was nothing. I took the instructor aside after class and explained to her that as I had been in a mental hospital I had had to endure being restrained and placed in a locked ward at one point so I was not comfortable having that done to me again. She said she would speak with her supervisors and mine and get back to me. Now this happened on the third day of orientation and the next day, which was a Friday, I was ambushed. I was taken by one of the case managers to the office of the person who supervised staff development. I was not told where I was going or what would happen when I got there. When we walked into the office not only was the staff development supervisor there but so were my unit supervisor and my direct supervisor. I was told to sit down and all of these people told me in no uncertain terms that I would submit to this demand and that I would do it in class in front of everyone or I would be fired on the spot. I explained that as I was hired under the auspices of DARS that I was entitled to a hearing with my therapist and counselor before anything was decided, that this was the law. They refused my request and I was fired on the spot. I was devastated. I have never been fired from a job in my life especially without due process. I even went to my DARS counselor and explained what had happened and asked her to intervene on my behalf, which is part of her job by the way, and she never did anything. In fact the interview and job I got all on my own without their help at all. I called and complained and still she did nothing and her supervisors did nothing to help me. I should have gone to the equal employment commission, but I was so devastated that I did not have the wherewithal to fight any further. This was just my first try at returning to work. I took a few days off to get over this blow and the next week I was right back at it again. I am stubborn if nothing else; maybe that is what has helped me get over set back after setback and continue on anyway.

I continued filling out job applications every week for all kinds of jobs within the human service sector, but it was not until the next January that I even got interviews again. I must have had 10 or 15 interviews and still no job offers. During this time I even had a teaching interview; boy was I psyched about that. Of course I did not get the job and for one simple reason I walked in carrying a cane. Now if I could prove this was the reason that I was denied the job then I could have taken my case to the Equal Employment Opportunity Commission (EEOC), but the problem was that I could not prove it I did not get the position. Lesson number two learned even if you can do the job do not show up with a wheelchair or a cane, or the powers that be will disqualify you. When I think about this obstacle keeping me from getting a job I get mad all over again. After all, these people that are interviewing me know the barriers put in the way of the people that we worked with and yet they did not hesitate to place the same barriers to my getting a job!

After discovering that I could not show any kind of disability and still hope to get a professional job, I began my search again. Although I was working with an employment counselor hired through DARS, any help I got was due entirely to my own work. I continued filling out applications right and left and still no bites. Finally it happened there were several openings with MHMR of Travis County. It seems they were looking for several case managers all at once. In fact they needed 16 by the first of June. The real kicker was that they wanted at least two case managers who were fluent in ASL. This job seemed tailor made for me. I had nothing to lose so I applied for all 16 positions hoping I would perhaps get at least one interview. The very next day I got a call and the following Monday I had an interview. Even though Austin has a large deaf community there are still a limited number of people who can actually sign fluently. I was offered the job that same week and I began work on April 27th. It seems that the state had passed a law that private agencies that ran community homes for the intellectually disabled could no longer police themselves by providing their own case managers. One of the jobs of the case managers is to see that all programs that are put in place by a team of people are carried out and all of the individual's needs are met. In the past all of these functions were carried out by the team hired by the private agency themselves. The parents of these providers would often neglect the needs of their client's. The case managers, who worked for the agency in question, followed the dictates of the agency rather than the individual. Thus, the new case manager positions were created for proper oversight by the state.

The state had set-up guidelines for the job in question, but no real wok had been done on how to train someone for a job that had never been done by the state before. Therefore, my first week I was given an office and a manual to read and no other instructions. It was not until a couple of weeks before June 1st, the date our job officially began, that we actually started working up a list of clients for each case manager. As I was the only person who could sign, anyone who was deaf was given to me. This meant that my client list changed from minute to minute and the area I had to cover in the county was larger than anyone else. The constant changing of my case load began to get on my nerves as I did not know what my job actually entailed or who I was to serve. I was anxious enough starting a new career after being on disability for five years. I actually thought that I would get a job and things would be as they were before. I did not take into account that just getting up and going to work every day would be stress enough in itself.

Each day I would leave my home two or more hours before I had to be at work because I was still riding the bus back and forth. On top of that stress was the fact that I had to have a car to do my job. When I accepted the position they knew I did not have a car, but I had to promise to get one by June 1st so I could make home visits, which was at least half of my job. I was excited to think of having my own car again, not to mention being able to afford to pay my own way. This felt like the last step to becoming my own person again. What I did not take into account was the added pressure all of these responsibilities would bring. I was feeling these pressures slowly build and yet I did not talk about them to anyone. It is still uncomfortable for me to talk about these issues because they are wrapped up with my feelings of self-worth and success. Our society trains us not to talk about these things because then we are somehow a failure. At the same time if I told any group of adults about my feelings of pressure and failure almost everyone would at least admit to having some of those same feelings. When did it become normal to not feel anything to be a successful adult? We all recognize those feelings in ourselves and others and yet we are constantly, from childhood, taught not to talk about them as if our feelings were shameful things.

Well, the pressure began to increase as the time came closer to start my job, for real. It came to a head a week or so after the entire office traveled to Fort Worth for a statewide training seminar. As I mentioned above the state had not been in charge of the case management process before so they were sort of making things up as they went along. In addition they had people trying to teach the job duties and responsibilities to a group of people who had not done this job before, and the presenters had no clue how to teach a group of people anything.

All the people in our group sat together each day going through PowerPoint after PowerPoint; at the end of it we had learned nothing and the presenters had only succeeded in frustrating and scaring the hell out of all of us. A good portion of what we had to learn to navigate were various computer programs that we had never heard of before and were antiquated at best. Trying to teach someone to use a computer program without actually navigating through it yourself is nearly impossible, unless you are a computer geek. If I had taught like that my supervisors would have thrown me out on my head. Yet the supervisors of this program continued to throw information at us expecting us to understand what they were talking about. As far as I could see most of our direct supervisors did not know how to use the information either.

As a group we were so confused and frustrated that by the end of the week we were all ready to just walk out the door. Yet the following Monday was June 1st, at which time were we finished with our so called training and starting our jobs without supervision. One of my issues was that on Monday we were to have introduction letters ready to send out to everyone on our caseload. The problem with that was I had all of the deaf clients and my case load kept changing from one minute to the next. Also we were to call all of the families and start setting up home visits. Everyone on our case load was to be seen at least once a month. I was originally told at most I would have 30 clients, but I ended up with 45. Home visits were just a part of our job; there were also staffing to set goals at least once a year as well as other duties. I was afraid that I would not be able to do my job and also frustrated that I did not understand what all I should be doing and was getting no support.

That Monday I woke up to go to work in a panic. I finally calmed myself by going through my morning routine, and then drove myself to work. I got my letter written and ready to send out and had addressed all of my envelopes when once again my supervisor came in and changed some of my caseload. This meant I had to change my list and all the information in my data base yet again. I finally got myself through all of that and after lunch I planned to start contacting families to set up meetings. I am normally an outgoing person and making contact with people is one of my strengths, but I was feeling so overwhelmed that when I started to pick up the phone and make contact I had a panic attack. It took me 30 minutes or more for me to calm down enough to make that first call. That first call kind of broke the ice and I was able to make several calls and appointments that day. Then just before I left for the day my caseload was changed again.

I was so stressed out that I did not sleep all night. By 5:00 that morning I knew I could not go to work so I called in. I thought calling in would help, but I became even more panicked and called my older sister, hysterical on the phone. She came over and with her help I called my therapist and he stayed on the phone with me for some time until I felt a little safer. Later that day I went to see him and we talked about my feeling so panicked. I went to work the next day and talked with my supervisor about my stress. My feelings of panic would abate for a few minutes, but when faced with a new maybe what most would consider a small challenge they returned full force. I could not sleep and at times I could not even function and I would have to hide in the restroom at work, having crying jags. Adding to my stress was the fact that I had just signed a note in order to get a car. If I quit I would have no way to pay for it. This went on for me for more than a week until I finally quit. My therapist assured me this stress and panic were my body remembering what I had gone through when I had quit working in 2004. He assured me this was a natural process and if I would be able to work through my feelings of panic and still be able to keep my job. Of course those feelings were so strong I was sure they would never stop so I quit and ran away from my panic. Anyone who has ever gone through a full panic attack would know that it truly feels as if you are going to die. My adrenaline would kick in and I would find myself in full fight or flight mode. It only became worse, when I realized that to everyone around me everything seemed normal. In addition I had to act as if I were not in a constant state of panic. I wish I had believed my therapist that I needed to confront and deal with my feelings of panic to move on, because when I eventually returned to work a lot of those feelings returned and had to be dealt with. My therapist told me after I quit he thought It would take me some time to move forward again. I am a very determined woman and by the next week I started searching for a job again. So in August I was working again. Granted it was not the job I wanted but as I was determined to keep my car I took the position. Although I have changed jobs a couple of times I have continued to work at least part time. I have had several problems to address as I continued working; however I have not quit because of panic. As my therapist promised me the panic has subsided as I have confronted each problem put in my path. A problem that continues for me is that no one will hire me for a professional teaching position despite my excellent credentials. It is still my goal to return to a professional position, hopefully in education, but I now realize that in order to prove myself I will have to pursue a graduate degree.

Erased

To be erased is to be
so eradicated it is as if
the person, place or event
had never existed.

To be blank is to be
empty to have nothing
nothing written or drawn there
void.

To have ones memories
erased is to be so void and
empty that nothing remains.
No taste, no smell, no sound,
no sense in any form that
something is even missing
to never have even been
a thought.

What do you do
if the essence
of who you were
is erased?

Do you then become
null and void?

What then do I do to find my mooring?
A place from which
I can plant myself
and begin to grow anew
if all that I am all that I have been
is erased.

Descent

Chapter 8

The Real Damage

Recent memory loss [produced by ECT] could be compared to erasing a tape recording.

Robert E. Arnot (1916-), "Observations on the Effects of Electric Convulsive Treatment in Man-Psychological," *Diseases of the Nervous System*, September 1975(1)

One day about a year after I had finished my ECT my older sister and I struck up a conversation about the weather being so hot outside. My younger sister and her partner had to be away from home for an extended time that day and they asked us to go to their home to let their dogs out in the yard and back into the house. I could not understand why they would not just let her dogs stay outside when they were gone. After all when I had been living with my younger sister she and I left our dogs outside when we were gone for an extended time. My older sister said, "Don't you remember? This sentence soon became a kind of sad mantra between me and my family. I looked at her blankly as I obviously had no idea to what she referred to. Then my older sister proceeded to tell me the story of how my Dad's dog had died under similar circumstances. While I was still living with my younger sister my Dad became ill and evidently we had to take care of his pug. Since we left our dogs outside we left his pug outside with them. When we arrived home the pug had died, presumably from the heat. When my older sister told me this story I started an argument with her. She had to be mistaken as I had absolutely no memory of this incident. My sister eventually stopped trying to convince me otherwise and dropped the subject. Several days later I was talking with my younger sister and related the story my older sister had told me. I just knew she would tell me that she had made the whole story up for some reason I could not fathom. My younger sister said in fact everything my older sister had told me was true. I was just dumbstruck. I could not believe that such an event could have happened and I had <u>absolutely</u> no memory of it.

While I am quite sure this type of memory loss had happened to me many times since electroshock therapy this is my first clear recollection of a missing memory from the time I was ill. At first when this happened I would argue with who ever told me. I know all people have various things they lose in the files of their memory; however this kind of memory loss is much more profound. Usually it is one or two things about an incident or time frame that gets misplaced or remembered in a different way. This type of loss is much more and not simply because a memory is gone. It's as if that entire time frame never even existed. Something more fundamental is lost because it involves not only whole periods of time but also erases all feeling and sensations, all connection of anyone or anything for that part of your life. For me it felt and continues to feel as if I never existed for that period of time. I can tell you most of my life story and how I felt until I come to one of these gaps and then I feel afloat in a dark space where I have no sensations, no substance at all. I don't know how else to explain it to anyone who has not undergone such a profound loss of self. I also lost connections to my work history although I have managed to regain some of that. Memories for the time I was under the influence of psychotropic drugs and electroshock treatments were not the only ones lost. I have come to realize I have lost chunks of childhood and adult memories from long before the time of my so called "treatments."

Electroshock has also affected the way I think and learn. For a long time after electroshock therapy I was much like a person who had had a stroke. I was unable to speak or write coherent thoughts. I had thoughts, but I either could not recall the word I needed or what I put on paper was not at all what I was thinking and often made no sense at all. I would know in my head what I wanted to say and I could even, sometimes define the word, but I could not find the word in my memory. In people with closed head injury or stroke they call this aphasia. I had to develop a whole strategy to deal with this deficit. At first I just became angry and fought against this, but after I began dealing with my grief over this and so much more, I worked to find a way to deal with my new challenges. I still at times feel anger and grief about these new "challenges," but I now realize that getting stuck in my anger and grief was not helping me or anyone else and in the end I would lose. First I recognized this learning disability shows up when I am speaking with another person or writing and is worse when I am tired or stressed, second when I recognize this is happening I stop and take a deep breath. Most of the people in my life know of this issue so when I am with them it is easier to deal with because I feel comfortable describing the word I am searching for and they will help fill in the blank for me. I am also fluent in American Sign Language as well as spoken English and since ASL is a visual concept language, it is easier at times to sign the word I mean. One of the problems with this is that some of my close family and friends understand me but not many others; still it can get me past the blank spot. Now that I am going out in public and speaking, I have to accept that sometimes the word I am searching for is not there and fill in as best as I can. At that point I have to try to let go of my embarrassment and frustration. If this does happen, unless someone who knows me very well is in the audience no one is even aware of my problem. The only person distressed is me, although I know the problem is not of my making, I am left to deal with it.

When I began writing I not only had a problem finding words in my memory but also when the words made it onto paper and I reread them it made little sense. What helped best with improving my writing was simply time to recover and the writing itself. It was and is hard to accept that something I was good at doing before, communicating using words, had deserted me. The thing is in some ways I still have difficulty with word recall, my writing in some ways is better for my experiences. My therapist suggested I start writing my story even when no one else read what I wrote; just the act of putting pen to paper helped me have a voice, so to speak. That is how this book came about.

The thing you never know is what memories are missing until you bump up against a blank spot. Many times I have met someone while out somewhere and they start talking to me about something we have done together and I either don't remember the person or the event which he/she is describing. After I started rebuilding my support community this happened to me several times. I rejoined a feminist group that I had been a part of before being subjected to ECT and drugs. One weekend I was invited to go to a writing retreat. The retreat center was owned and run by one of the ladies in our group. I had re-met her and the other women several months earlier. Most of the women in this group knew what I had gone through and about my memory problems. When I arrived at the center I thought it was a beautiful place. After I settled in I walked the lovely labyrinth located there. That evening about an hour before dinner, the woman who owned the center drew me over to the window where she had two chairs. We sat and for the next hour we watched the birds eating from the feeders on the back porch. While we were bird watching she reminded me this was not my first visit to this retreat center. I pretended as best I could that I remembered what she was talking about; I did not want to explain my whole story yet again. However, the next day the whole group of women were discussing what we were writing about and reading from our writing. I told my story to the group and talked about having my memory erased by electroshock. The woman I had been watching the birds with told me her parents had subjected her to ECT to "shock" her out of being a lesbian. After that all of the women in this group knew that I often did not remember events or people they were talking about and they even went out of the way to make sure I knew what or who they were referring to. It is now just accepted in this group of women that when I meet someone they tell me if I knew them previously. At least in this circle of sister women I do not have to pretend that I have not lost a good portion of my memory. At this point I know I have recovered as much of my memory as I am likely to and from now forward I have ways of compensating for my new challenges.

Unfortunately my story of injury from psychiatry does not end with just memory loss. There are also illnesses and injuries inflicted by the many psychiatric drugs I ingested. There were many drugs starting with the anti-depressant Paxil. As I previously stated, it was initially prescribed to me by my primary care physician when I complained about pain from arthritis and fibromyalgia. I took the Paxil for about a year when I had surgery on my right foot that took a long time to heal. At that point I became depressed and my doctor increased my dosage of Paxil. Having no idea of the side effects of such drugs I did not connect my worsening depression to the drug; after all this drug was supposed to help not hurt me. Of course only a few weeks or days, I am truly not sure which, I later took my first overdose of pills. After I was released from the psychiatric hospital that first time I was taking seven psychotropic drugs. During the entire time I was medicated, I took many different drugs, each with their own side effects. Each time I was admitted to the hospital, a total of nine times in all, many within a few days or weeks of being released, my drugs were changed or dosages upped and my condition continued to deteriorate both physically and emotionally. Each time the psychiatrist would change my drug cocktail and or increase the dosages I was told that my worsening condition was due to the disease process, and that this proved that I had been correctly diagnosed and labeled with the mental illness of Bipolar Depression. Eventually the right combination of drugs would be found and then I would have to remain on them for the rest of my life. At no time was it suggested that the drugs were making me chronically ill.

After my last admission to Shoal Creek in July of 2007 I left the hospital with a reduced number of drugs and at minimal dosages, at my own request, a thing that previously would never have occurred to me. This drug change caused me to have two serious reactions though I was unaware of these side effects until I was rushed to the hospital with a possible heart attack. The first of the side effects was a loss of bladder control. The second and more serious side effect was heart palpitation. As it turns out these were the most easily correctable problems that occurred due to the psychiatric drugs. Both effects were caused by Geodon, so my antipsychotic was changed and in a few days both issues began to resolve themselves. There were, of course, more serious health problems that were directly caused by the psychiatric drugs I was taking.

The first serious problem I developed was weight gain. Although I did not realize it at the time this is a well-known side effect of a lot of the drugs I was taking. My weight went from 250, already a significant weight, to 300 pounds in a matter of a few months. I don't understand all of the reasons for weight gain of such a significant amount in a short period of time, but I know it is a common effect and that permanent metabolic damage often occurs regularly in the form of Diabetes. What I can say is that at times I would not want anything to eat; at other times I was constantly hungry. I would crave sweets or other foods like popcorn and eat only those foods. Needless to say this sudden weigh change caused many problems. I was unable to walk very well and my arthritis and fibromyalgia became worse. My breathing and allergies became chronic problems and I had one illness after the other. If someone got the flu I contracted it as well. I had always had bronchial problems, but I got bronchitis so often I was diagnosed with COPD. Secondary to that my blood sugars went haywire, a condition which is known to cause or worsen depression in itself. The main drug I was taking that is known not only to throw off your blood sugar but can cause diabetes and pancreatitis is Seroquel. Seroquel is known to cause damage to the pancreas which can lead to the above listed conditions. I did not develop pancreatitis but eventually developed diabetes. I will have to take medication and alter my diet for the rest of my life due to this condition even though I have since lost more than 90 pounds. The psychiatrists know many drugs have this feature as a side effect, yet when I showed signs of these problems I was not taken off of this drug.

The third condition I developed was thyroid nodules and eventually thyroid cancer while taking the drug Lamictal. This effect is so widely known by psychiatrists that when a patient is taking this drug they are sent for ultrasound tests every six months. I took this drug from my first hospitalization in September of 2004 until July of 2007 when I told my psychiatrist that I wanted to stop taking it. In this entire time frame I was never told of this effect of the drug and was never sent for an ultrasound test even once. In 2006 I was diagnosed with underactive thyroid and started taking synthroid to increase my hormone output. Even at that no one told me that Lamictal was likely damaging my thyroid. I continued having problems breathing, especially when I lay down. Finally I asked to be sent to an endocrinologist as I now had been diagnosed with diabetes as well as thyroid disease. I was sent for an ultrasound at which time I was told I had two nodules on my thyroid. I was then scheduled for a biopsy to see if either nodule was cancerous. I arrived at the hospital just to be told to go home. The doctor said one nodule was too small to be cancerous and the other was too large. The endocrinologist said I could live with the nodules or he would refer me to a surgeon. I went to the surgeon and although there was no indication of cancer we decided the nodules were impeding my swallowing and breathing so I decided to have my thyroid removed. The surgery took longer than anticipated because the nodes were so large that the surgeon had trouble getting the breathing tube down my throat. After the surgery the tissue they removed was tested for cancer and indeed they found a tumor, much to the surprise of everyone involved. So now I am checked yearly for thyroid cancer and I have to take hormones for the rest of my life. The issues did not end with the removal of my thyroid and the taking of a drug. The thyroid gland sends out hormones that help control everything related to the endocrine system and thus regulates things such as blood pressure and insulin production.

There is nothing so clear to anyone as hindsight. After I stopped ECT treatment and started withdrawing from psychotropic drugs I began to do research into the various drugs and their effects. The truth to me was frightening and one of the reasons I decided to speak out about my treatment. It was also difficult to find out about the real side effects of the various drugs I took during my "treatment." The interactions between all the various drugs, includes the psychotropic drugs and the blood pressure and thyroid and blood sugar regulating drugs; is almost impossible to know as no one really tracks that. For that reason among many others it became paramount for me to know what I was putting in my body and what effects they would have. Below I have listed all of the psychotropic drugs I took during the years I was being "treated" by psychiatry and as many of the side effects as I could find. As I have said it is nearly impossible to know the interactions between the various drugs. I am by no means unique in the amount and variety of drugs that were given to me, but I hope it will serve to illustrate my point that we all need to understand what we are being given and find out for ourselves what we are putting in our bodies. I believe the greater portion of responsibility lies with the psychiatric industry and all who are involved to look at what harm these drugs do; however, the industry as it stands will not change unless we start with ourselves and then work to educate others. To this end I have dedicated myself. The information below is taken from *The Pill Book 14th Edition* edited by Harold M. Silverman, pharm. D. (2)

Depakote, Dilantin, Lamictal, Neurotin

Anticonvulsants were developed for seizure disorders, but are also prescribed for "bipolar disorder."

Depakote: nausea, vomiting diarrhea, abdominal pain, dizziness, indigestion, sedation or sleepiness, weakness, weight gain, emotional upset, depression, constipation, increased or decreased appetite, change in menstrual periods, headache, double vision, loss of muscle control or coordination and or tremors. Usual dosage: 125-750mg depending on body weight. Doses of 250 or less at bedtime. My dosage:500mg at bedtime(1192).

Dilantin: drowsiness, slurred speech, mental confusion, nystagmus (rhythmic, uncontrolled movement of the eye), dizziness, insomnia, nervousness, uncontrollable twitching, double vision, tiredness, irritability, depression, tremors, and headache, nausea, vomiting, diarrhea, constipation, weight gain, bronchitis, sensitivity to bright light, high blood sugar, and liver damage. Usual dosage: 300 to 400 mg a day with a maximum of 600 mg a day. My dosage: 1000 mg per day (881).

Lamictal: headache, dizziness, nausea vomiting, weakness, tiredness, loss of coordination, double vision, blurred vision, dental problems, sleeplessness, tremors, depression, anxiety, convulsions, irritability, chills, hot flashes, dry mouth, joint ache, sore throat, memory loss, confusion breathing difficulties, ear pain, ringing in the ears. Usual dosage: Maximum allowed is 500 mg depending on other seizure medication being taken. My dosage: started at 100mg at bedtime, decreased to 50 mg at bedtime, increased again to 150 mg at bedtime, then finally to 100 mg three times a day (629).

Neurotin: tiredness, dizziness, edema in legs and arms, fatigue, double vision, tremors, weight gain, upset stomach, dry mouth, dental problems, muscle aches, sore throat, speech problems, memory loss, depression, abnormal thinking, twitching, itching, visual disturbances, increased appetite, poor coordination, low red and white blood cell counts(1121).

Paxil, Zoloft

(SSRIs) Selective Serototin Reuptake Inhibitors, developed and given for a number of psychiatric disorders. There are several SSRIs, which generally have the same side effects as they are essentially the same drug. The two I ingested are Paxil and Zoloft.

Paxil, Zoloft: headache, anxiety, nervousness, sleeplessness, drowsiness, tiredness, weakness, tremors, night sweats, dizziness, lightheadedness, dry mouth, upset stomach, appetite loss or gain, nausea, vomiting, diarrhea, weight loss or gain, electric-shock sensations, difficulty concentrating, dizziness, bronchitis, blood pressure changes, body aches, low blood sugar, and low thyroid activity. Usual dosage Paxil: 20-60 mg a day or 25-75 for Paxil CR. My dosage Paxil: 37.5 then changed to CR and upped to 50 mg per day. Usual dosage Zoloft: 25-200 mg a day with usual dose at 50 mg per day. My dosage Zoloft: started at 100 mg, later increased to 150 mg per day (1113).

Geodon, Lithium, Seroquel

Antipsychotic drugs are used for schizophrenia, bipolar, and mania.

Geodon: sleepiness, nausea, weakness, rapid heartbeat, dizziness, diarrhea, restlessness, dry mouth, muscle aches, rigid muscles, loss of bladder control. Usual dosage: 20-100 twice a day. My dosage: 100 mg twice a day (1227).

Lithium: fine hand tremor, thirst, excessive urination, nausea, vomiting, drowsiness, diarrhea, muscle weakness and poor coordination, affect muscles and nerves, stomach, intestines, kidneys and urinary tract as well as thyroid function. Usual dosage: 300 mg 3-4 times a day. My dosage: 300 mg am and 600 mg pm (656).

Seroquel: dizziness, headache, agitation, upset stomach, dizziness, weight gain, dry mouth, swelling in the arms or legs, spastic movements, sore throat, breathing difficulties, heart palpitations, body aches, low white-blood cell counts, high blood sugar, diabetes. Usual dosage: starting dose 300 mg and increased to 400-800 mg a day for bipolar disorder. My dosage: started at 100 mg increased first to 300 mg then 400 mg and finally to 600 mg at bedtime (931).

Ambien

Sedative given for insomnia

Ambien: headache, drowsiness, dizziness, lightheadedness, nausea, diarrhea, fatigue, unusual dreams, memory loss, anxiety, nervousness, difficulty sleeping, appetite loss, vomiting, body aches, depression, dry mouth, upper respiratory infection, urinary infection, heart palpitations, walking, eating or even driving in your sleep. Usual dosage: 10 mg immediately before bedtime. My dosage: 10 mg immediately before bedtime (1231).

Ativan, Xanax

Benzodiazepine sedative, prescribed mostly for anxiety, tension, and panic attacks

Ativan   (Lorazepam):   drowsiness,   weakness, confusion, depression, lethargy, confusion, headache, slurred speech, dry mouth, nausea, loss of bowel control,   nervousness,   hysteria,   psychosis, sleeplessness, liver dysfunction. Usual dosage: 2-40 mg per day. My dosage: 2mg at bedtime (372).

Xanax: drowsiness, weakness, confusion, depression, lethargy, headache, slurred speech, dizziness, tremors, dry mouth, nausea, loss of bladder control, low blood pressure, fluid retention, blurred vision, nervousness, sleeplessness,   liver   dysfunction,   hallucinations, depersonalization (loss of sense of personal identity. Usual dosage: Anxiety Disorder 0.25-0.5 mg three times a day with a maximum of four times a day. Panic Disorder 1-10 mg a day. My dosage: started 0.1 mg twice a day later increased to three times a day (62).

Klonopin

Anticonvulsant, developed for seizure control but also prescribed for schizophrenia, mania and anxiety

Klonopin: drowsiness, poor muscle control, and behavioral changes, mental function, stomach and intestinal problems, urinary, blood and liver disorders. Usual dosage: Panic Attacks started at 0.25 increased to usual dosage of 1 mg with maximum of 4 mg twice daily. My dosage: started 0.5 mg twice a day and increased to 1 mg three times a day (274).

These above listings include only the side effects and not the various interactions that are known with many of the above listed drugs. These drugs also tend to be highly addictive, and are often very difficult to discontinue, with a range of withdrawal symptoms that can be severe.

These drugs were just the psychotropic drugs I took and do not include the drugs for blood pressure, thyroid function and blood sugar regulation. There were also the various drugs that were given to me during ECT. If you will look at the various side effects many are listed with most if not all of the above classes of drugs. I can tell you without reservation that I experienced most of the ones that are repeated in each of the lists above. I also experienced many of the not so typical effects such as behavioral changes and, loss of memory and mental function as well as auditory and visual hallucinations which I had never experienced before or since. You might notice also several list worsening of depression and anxiety, which was the issue that I complained about at the beginning. Yet when I told my psychiatrist of any of these issues I was told it was part of my disease process and was never once considered by any of the various "doctors" as possible side effects. This of course did not even begin to include the other physical problems that cropped up like chronic bronchitis, low white-blood and red-blood cell counts as well as low potassium and liver functions being off and any number of other issues which were always considered unrelated. As I had never had any experience with psychiatric treatment before it was little wonder that I did not realize what was causing many of my problems; however, it is impossible for me to believe that my psychiatrist had no knowledge that many if not most of my physical, mental, and emotional problems were due in no small part to the drugs he told me I must take for the rest of my life. No matter what you think of the psychiatric system this deliberate disregard of glaring facts is too much for anyone to swallow unless they take plenty of mind numbing drugs as I did and are kept in a confused and compliant state, as I was .

Descent

Reemerging
Coming out, rebirth
Once upon a time I was hurt physically and emotionally
by many things. I felt low
and worthless as a caterpillar. Then
just like a caterpillar I drew
within myself and built a
cocoon as protection against
the world. From hurt, fear
and a hostile world. I built
a cocoon so solid and thick
that no one could see me or hear
me not even myself

In the dark of my cocoon
I took my fear out on myself
Later, with help I began transmuting
my fear. Instead of consuming myself
in the dark I began transforming
myself instead.

When I had
transformed enough of my fear
to strength I broke once more
through the walls of my self
imposed cocoon. Just like the
caterpillar that transformed herself
into a butterfly.

Descent

Chapter 9

The Heroine's Birth

The modern hero, the modern individual who dares to heed the call and seek the mansion of that presence with whom it is our whole destiny to be atoned, cannot indeed must not, wait for his community to cast off its slough of pride, fear, rationalized avarice, and sanctified misunderstanding. "Live," Nietzsche says "as though the day were here." It is not society that is to guide and save the creative hero, but precisely the reverse. And so every one of us shares the supreme ordeal-carries the cross of the redeemer-not in the bright moments of his tribe's great victories, but in the silences of his personal despair.

Joseph Campbell (1904-1987), *Closing words, The Hero with a Thousand Faces,* 1949(1)

My rebirth began with my descent though I was too overwhelmed by drugs and what psychiatrists were telling me was a "dis-ease" to notice. There is an ancient Sumerian myth of two goddesses one named Inanna, goddess of heaven and the other named Ereshkigal goddess of the underworld. Inanna and Ereshkigal were sisters and each sister's personality was a mirror image of the other. This ancient story tells that Inanna descended to the underworld to attend the funeral of Ereshkigal's husband. Before descending to the underworld Inanna told her loyal servant that if she did not return in three days to go to the father Gods and ask them for help. As Inanna descended to the underworld she must pass through seven gates with seven guards. At each gate she removed a piece of clothing and jewelry until she arrived clad in only her skin. Inanna arrived and offered to comfort her sister Ereshkigal. Ereshkigal felt her sister was unable to understand her feelings of grief so she struck out at Inanna and killed her then hung her on a peg on the wall. While going through the depression and ECT and drugs I totally lost all concept of myself all parts of my personality were literally stripped away. I did not know who or what I was any longer; in fact I felt as if I had truly died. The descent of Inanna mirrored to me the path I took into my own underworld. My sister did not kill me with her grief; instead I did that to myself and then drew a cocoon around myself in order to protect myself from any further hurt.

When Inanna did not return in three days her servant went to the father Gods to plead for help in rescuing her from the underworld. Two of the father Gods refused to help her and sent the servant away. Their reasoning was to blame her for trying to help her sister. This feels to me like what happened to me in my search for help. First I was told that I had a disease and that they, the benevolent psychiatrists, could treat me but not truly help or cure, for the fault was mine. I had long ago learned the lesson that everything was my fault so I believed what they told me and just continued to take my grief out on myself just as Ereshkigal took her grief out on her sister. Inanna and Ereshkigal were the two sides of myself trying to come to terms with each other in a natural process called emotional growth, but that process was halted by the drugs and ECT that were prescribed for me. I hung myself on the hook and pulled the cocoon in around myself trying to protect myself from my grief. I hung there in that black hole and flayed myself literally and figuratively because I had no idea what else to do.

When we look at what happened for the two sisters Inanna and Ereshkigal, we see the mirror of what happened to me as well. Inanna's trusted servant did not give up with the first two father Gods and went to the third and last father God to beg for help. He listened to Inanna's servant and in his compassion took dirt from under his nails and created two sexless creatures to go to the underworld to rescue Inanna. The two creatures being sexless, were able to sneak into the underworld unseen by the guards at the gates. The two creatures listened to Ereshkigal's story of grief. They did not try to talk her out of her grief or blame her for any of her actions; they just sat and listened and grieved her loss with her. After a time Ereshkigal was able to let go of some of her grief and then she saw what she had done to her sister Inanna. Ereshkigal gave the creatures the food and water of life and allowed them to feed Inanna until she recovered. My older sister did not give up looking for ways to help me and talked to anyone who would listen to her. Finally she found the man who eventually became my therapist. My older sister performed the same feat for me that Inanna's loyal servant did for her. She found someone that could come down into the underworld with me and listen to me. My therapist just listened without judgment to what had happened to me. For me the process of recovery was and is a long arduous process. Only when I was able to let go of my grief and fear was I able to see clearly what had happened to me. When I realized what psychiatry had done to me I became angry and that was the point at which I became alive again and started to crawl out of my cocoon.

When Inanna finally began her long walk out of the underworld she re-clothed herself. However when she emerged she had changed in subtle ways. Inanna was not the same woman she was when she descended. When I began my long walk out I had found that I lost much of my old self. Some of those pieces I found along the way and some I found no longer served me so I discarded. When I discarded the pieces of my clothing that were out of date I found I could replace them with stronger attributes that served me in much more positive ways. The strongest attribute I found was my voice and I am strengthening it every day with every word I use.

Much like a butterfly after emerging from its cocoon I had to sit while my wings dried and my advocate muscles became stronger. Exercising my muscles was at first a slow cautious process. The first time I spoke to anyone was when my older sister talked me into going to the CCHR office and video tape an interview which was posted on YouTube psyche truth channel, and is also in the video archives at www.endofshock.org. It took my sister several days to talk me into going to the office and speaking on camera about what had happened to me. Several weeks went by after that first foray into public speaking before I again went out and this time spoke to a large crowd of people, described in detail in chapter 7. This was the first time I had ever spoken to a large group. This group was comprised of folks who had, been through the same psychiatric system themselves, or someone close to them had and so they were eager to hear anyone speak in public against the psychiatric system as it is set up today. I don't remember what I said but the crowd cheered when I spoke and that gave my ego a much needed boost so that when I was asked to speak again I was more than willing. After the event there was a write up about the event in the paper. Just reading about all of the people who had survived the abuse of electroshock made me feel for the first time in a long time like I was part of something that was positive. I felt I was part of a group again and not separate from the world.

Our Coalition for the Abolition of Electroshock in Texas (CAEST) then asked me to speak before the Austin City Council. I was allowed only 3-5 minutes to speak. I carefully wrote out what I wanted to say. I even practiced reading my speech at home several times. It was necessary for me to write out what I wanted to say and practice reading it to my sister because although I knew in my head what I wanted to say my words still got mixed up and often did not make sense. Putting my thoughts in coherent order on paper was still a challenge for me although with repetition and practice this was becoming easier. I still have problems with it though especially when I am tired and nervous or stressed. I have lost the copy of the full statement I made but I did use the following quote by Leonard Roy Frank, "The prime purpose of psychiatric treatments...whether utilizing drugs, electric surgery, or confinement especially if imposed on unconsenting clients...is to authenticate the subject as a "patient," the psychiatrist as a "doctor," and the intervention as a "treatment". The cost of this fictionalization runs high. It requires the sacrifice of the patient as a person the psychiatrist as a critical thinker and moral agent, and of the legal system as a protector of the citizens against the abuse of state power."(2) As far as I can tell all of the speeches to the City Council fell on deaf ears, but that has yet to stop me from speaking my truth. Just like all of the now famous revolutionaries, their words were ignored until enough people who believed it came together to make a difference. It is my hope that I will one day, hopefully sooner than later, meet critical mass and we psychiatric survivors as a group will make a difference.

I was lucky in that I was able to find a place where others understood what I had gone through, and I knew that writing and speaking to others was a powerful way to help my reemergence. From that point on you could not stop me from trying to advocate for myself and others. What I had to work on and am still fine tuning is the most effective way to do that. At first I did not know how to find the resources I needed, but slowly with persistence I was able to find help for most of the things I needed. Things such as how to get Medicare to pay for a motorized wheelchair, how to get my apartment complex to fix the ramps so that I could use my wheelchair, and one of the most important doctors that actually listened to what I wanted for myself in the way of help.

This last piece of finding a doctor that listened took some time and several tries to get it right. One thing I found out is that you have a right and should interview your doctor during your initial visit. If they have a problem with that then find a different doctor. Next I had to learn how to talk to doctors and ask questions about what treatments I was willing to undergo and which I would not. If the doctor does not agree to this keep looking. I personally went through several doctors before I found a group of doctors that worked for me in a way I wanted. This was hugely an important part for me. For far too long I had just accepted, what a doctor of any kind prescribed without question. When I began to question my doctors and ask about other treatments and refusing some I of course ran into resistance. My doctors and I don't always agree, but at times when I refuse the treatment advised some of them have gone back and done research to find alternatives that we might agree on. One of the most important things I have come to realize is that even when they mean well doctors often don't have all of the information or research not touted by the mainstream (drug companies) so I don't mind teaching them my point of view. Four questions I always ask are: What is the goal of this treatment? How likely is this treatment to work? What are the side effects of this treatment? Are there alternative treatments? Then I do my own research into the various treatments before I make my decision. Before I learned to advocate for myself I never would have thought to do any of these things.

Even as I learned to advocate for myself and to speak at public meetings, etc. it never really occurred to me that writing my story would be helpful to anyone until encouraged by my therapist to do so. From the beginning I liked the idea of writing my story, but several issues hampered me. My story obviously involves more than just myself. I wanted to write the truth as I saw it, but did not want to hurt my family or friends. My current beliefs about psychiatry has put up some walls in personal relationships. I encourage anyone who wishes to speak their truth; just know that it will bring up issues between you and those who have different views. As with my personal relationships you may be able to get past this issue or work around it and then you may not. This was and is a critical issue for me in all of my personal relationships. It took me a while to work up the courage but in the end I had to tell my story as I remembered it.

That brings up the second issue that of my erased memory. How can I write my story if I don't remember most of it? My memory loss became an integral part of my story. After I began writing I often came upon a memory that caused me great distress and I had to work through my fears before I could continue. This was a good thing for me. Each time I dealt with my fears surrounding an issue or memory it released me from fear and I was able to then deal with the feelings behind the fear. This releasing allowed new possibilities to slowly fill up my life. This was and is probably the single best thing to come out of this whole episode in my life. After I began writing and speaking my life began to slowly change for the better. I was able to stop taking all psychotropic drugs by December of 2008 and with that and being able to work through my fears I was able to begin looking at the world with clear eyes and straight thinking.

My Dream

Several years ago I was
living my dream but...
then it broke.

Now on nights when
I toss and turn
I dare to have a dream again

I dream of teaching again.
I dream of helping those
who others have given up on.
I dream of telling my story
I dream of being heard
and making a difference

My dream may seem
small to some.
After all my dream
won't make me famous or
fill my pockets
with silver and gold
But my dream is large to me.
My dream will give me use.

My dream may seem small
to some, but
it gives me hope that
as my mother always told me
"You are big enough to do anything you think you can"
To me my dream is not small
and I am big enough.

Descent

Chapter 10

The Heroine's Return

"We have not even to risk the adventure alone for the hero's of all time have gone before us. The labyrinth is thoroughly known. We have only to follow the thread of the hero path. And where we had thought to find an abomination, we shall find a god. And where we had though to slay another, we shall slay ourselves. And where we had though to travel outward, we shall come to the center of our own existence. And where we had thought to be alone we shall be with all the world." *The Hero With A Thousand Faces,* Joseph Campbell (1)

Now I began to rebuild a support system with friends, family and community. I not only wrote, but continued to speak to issues about the psychiatric system. My therapist asked me if he could write an article about my experiences for a journal. I agreed but told him that I wanted him to use my real name, not a made up one to protect the innocent. We also decided to include the name of the psychiatrist who had treated me for so long. The writing of the article gave me courage to do one other thing, to at least on paper confront the psychiatrist who had caused me such harm. So I wrote a letter to Dr. Lam and sent it certified mail then I took that confrontation one step further. I made a video of me reading this letter to Dr. Lam and we published it on YouTube on the psychetruth channel. Eventually the article was approved by the Journal of Humanistic Psychology, and I am the coauthor. The very last thing my therapist and I decided to do was add my letter to Dr. Lam at the end of the article. This was agreed to by the journal only because I had previously published it on the web. The article was published on the Journal's website last year; the hard copy was published in the January 2012 issue, (53). (2) The following is the letter I sent to Dr. Lam.

Friday, February 26, 2010

Open letter to Dr. Lam:

When I met you at Seton Shoal Creek Hospital several years ago I was a vulnerable, desperate, confused woman. You and Shoal Creek were my first contact with psychiatry. I expected that you were there to help me overcome the emotional problems that were weighing me down. You were the doctor and I thought you were there to help. Instead of helping me you and all of your pills and electroconvulsive therapy in fact made me ill and very nearly destroyed me. Since leaving your care I have in fact found a real caring therapist who helped me heal myself and figure out a few things into the bargain.

First, I am not now and never was "mentally ill" because there is no biopsychiatric "mental illness" that caused my emotional upset. I did have serious physical medical problems with thyroid and blood sugar functions, which you and Shoal Creek chose to ignore and for which I later received help. Second, I do not need your pills and ECT treatments to "get better." I am a whole individual and there is nothing wrong with my mind. I only needed a place where it was safe for me to explore what issues were causing my emotional distress. Something your pills and treatments would never allow me, or anyone else for that matter, to do. Your brand of "treatment" only serves to shut down any healing and in effect shut-up anything your patients need to say.

I have gotten off of all of your drugs and healed as much as physically possible from the effects of your ECT treatments. I have found my voice again and I will not be silenced. Dr. Lam I am here to tell you and anyone else who will listen how dangerous you and your treatments are. My goal is to inform as many people as I can of the dangerous effects of all of your forms of help. You once asked me, "Don't you want to get better!" Now I can give you my answer. No!!! I say no because I have nothing to get better from as if I was ill or broken and only by following your orders would I "get better", but never well. As if everything that was happening to me was my fault and I was to blame for it all. I don't need fixing, only caring and understanding, two things you <u>never</u> showed me. A good friend of mine tells me that every time she sees you, you ask about me. In response I say stop. I don't even want that much of your so-called caring treatment.

Sincerely,

Evelyn Scogin

Psychiatric Survivor

Activist for Humanistic Psychiatry

In January of 2011, a historic event happened, and I played a part. The FDA was having a hearing in Washington D.C. about reclassifying electroshock machines. Electroshock treatments began to be used widely in the United States after WWII, prior to the development of the FDA. When the FDA began its work rather than do the appropriate testing to ensure the safety and efficacy of this controversial treatment they instead "grandfathered" in as a class III device. This classification meant that the device was considered experimental and that the manufacturers needed to prove efficacy and safety of the device. In the ensuing decades the FDA had never forced the manufacturers or psychiatrists using these devices and treatments to comply with this part of the rules. Then the psychiatrists and manufacturers of these machines started pushing the FDA to reclassify these machines as safe without proof. Those of us that have gone through this torture disguised as "treatment" have begun to band together with the help of groups like CAEST and CCHR, and to make our voices heard. So when the FDA decided to have a hearing on the issue I was asked by CCHR to go with them to speak directly to the group.

For me this became an even bigger event as I had to fly to Washington. This was exciting as well as frightening as I have a fear of flying. The trip turned into an ordeal in itself as there was a massive snowstorm going through the northeast United States at that time. In the end the group I was traveling with ended up stuck in the airport and never made it all the way to the hearing. Another of our group traveling independently actually made it to the hearing and had our testimonies read into the record. This is my testimony as read into the record.

Testimony Before FDA (2011)

My name is Evelyn Scogin and I am here today to tell you my story of assault from ECT so that you will understand the harm this machine does every time it is used. I came to psychiatry in 2004 at the age of 47. I was experiencing several stressors at the same time so I naturally turned to a mental health professional for assistance and advice.

I entered the psychiatric system at that time trusting the psychiatrist as the health professional that could care for me in my time of need and perhaps help me solve my emotional issues. At least that is what I was led to believe. I entered the hospital taking one psychiatric drug and left taking seven. My psychiatrist immediately diagnosed me with bipolar disorder. Four months later I had been in and out of the hospital at least three times and each time my drug cocktail was changed and dosages increased until at the end of the year I was on so many drugs I could no longer function.

At the urging of this same psychiatrist I gave up my hard won career of teaching special needs deaf students. One month later in January of 2005 I was again in the hospital because I was so depressed I had tried to commit suicide. He said I also had a borderline personality disorder and he accused me of not wanting to get well. The psychiatrist could not increase the dosages of the drugs I was taking or add more drugs for fear of killing me. The drugs were proving to be ineffective for my problems and thus he suggested ECT.

My sister has informed me that the psychiatrist described the treatment as safe with only a loss of memory for the day of the treatment and that would return shortly after. Being desperate and not knowing what else to do I agreed. I had always been led to believe that medical professionals only had my health in mind so I should follow the course of treatment that they suggested. Never did it occur to me that anything a so called health professional recommended would be harmful to me.

My sister had to tell me of the events that transpired because I have no memory of this meeting or all the events afterward. [PAUSE] I was subjected to six months and at least 30 so called treatments. During my course of treatment my emotional, physical and cognitive health severely declined. My sister stated that when I was released from the hospital after a treatment I often had urinated in my clothes and was sent home without changing. In addition I was unable to stand and walk out of the hospital and since they did not provide me with a wheelchair she would have to prop me up against various walls to assist getting me to the car. When I got in the car she would ask how I felt and I was always incoherent and often hallucinating. When I arrived home I would pass out for six or more hours and would remain incoherent for at least a day after.

I could not be left alone as I would wander off somewhere and become lost. I often could not tell you my name or the names of any of my family. I lost not only my memories of the time I was subjected to this torture but I was robbed of almost all memories from about 2003, two years before treatment, to 2008, three years after treatment stopped. I was unable to converse or write coherently because my word recall was so limited, just like someone who had, had a stroke would do. Taking care of many of my every day needs was beyond me. In fact one of my sisters had to take charge of my bank account. I could no longer drive or even go to the mail box alone. During these procedures all of my upper teeth were broken off and I have been unable to get the dental care I need. [PAUSE FOR EMPHASIS]

I have fought long and hard over the last four years to recover from the effects of this abuse and rebuild my life. I, however, will never recover the part of myself that was stolen from me with my memories. Even as I speak to you today I discover more and more learning difficulties and I still have problems recalling words at times. Because of these lasting effects I have as yet been unable to return to my chosen profession of teaching. I am training for a new job now but it remains a struggle for me each and every day to learn new tasks and relearn old ones.

My story is not a unique one. In fact it is sadly all too common. Until electro convulsive therapy is abolished I will continue to speak whenever and wherever I can. Until such a time at least force the manufacturers of these machines and purveyors of this treatment to prove their inefficacy and danger by going through the same trials as any other dangerous new medical device or treatment. Protect the people who turn to mental health professionals for help and receive only lies and abuse.

I was distressed over these turn of events, but I did face my fear of flying and came out okay at the time of the trip even though my luggage and medicine was lost for two days. In the end however, much to the surprise of all involved we actually won this round with the FDA panel. The electro shock machines and treatment remains at classification III. In addition the manufacturers and psychiatrists must now provide scientific proof that their machines and treatment are safe and effective. How long this will take or what form the research will take remains to be seen; now is the time we as ECT survivors need to work to make sure that the scientific community follows through with its promise.

This was my first time at seeing how our government regulatory agencies work. I thought the panel was one group of individuals appointed to the post and they held meetings for different drugs and treatments and that the same group of individuals served for a set period of time. What I found out was that there were many people on this panel pulled from different areas with interests related to the issues before the board. In other words there were psychiatrists and electroshock machine manufacturers, as well a neurologists and patient representatives. So the people who have the most interest in seeing that the issue be approved by the panel are themselves part of the voting process. This to me seemed to be a conflict of interest. The thing that tipped the vote in our favor was that the majority of the panel for once did not have a vested interest in seeing that electroshock machines be reclassified. For a detailed description of these events see "Battle at Gaithersburg" at www.endofshock.org.

Shortly after I returned from my trip I was asked to speak against a couple of bills being introduced to committees of the Texas legislature. Up until this point I had no real idea how bills were introduced into the legislature. It was an eye opener to me to see this process at work. The thing is anyone who has an interest in a bill being introduced to a committee can go speak for or against said bill. The legislature has a website that lists the bills coming up to be introduced to committee and when and where the committees will meet. When you arrive at the committee meeting they will have several bills up for consideration that day so you just have to sign up to be on the list to speak for or against that bill. The hardest part of the whole ordeal is to sit and wait until your bill is called to the floor; this can take many hours or just a few minutes, you never really know. When you are called to speak you have two or three minutes to talk, depending on how many people are speaking about that bill, they can and will cut you off mid-sentence. Trust me when I tell you that bills related to psychiatric practices always have a long list of people who wish to speak. Many of the people who speak are psychiatrists and people whose jobs are directly involved in these issues. CCHR is a great watchdog for issues of this kind and rallies the troops to speak when these bills are introduced. Some of the representatives on the committees listen more carefully to what you have to say than others, but I have never regretted using my right to free speech to try and educate the representatives to the other side of "mental health" issues.

The first bill that I spoke against was HB836 introduced in the 2011 legislature. One of the provisions of the bill states that persons who are labeled with a psychiatric diagnosis can be forced to take psychiatric drugs and counseling if they refuse treatment and their psychiatrist disagrees. The court could order that the "patient" be forced to take medication if they have been given a psychiatric diagnoses and refuses to take drugs if the doctor says they are likely to harm themselves or others, may be hospitalized within a few months or has been hospitalized involuntarily three time in the past eighteen months or five times in their entire life.

I don't know about the rest of you but I was shocked to find out I have a right to refuse all medical treatments even if I will die by doing so. In Texas the psychiatrists still have to go through a lengthy court process to take this right away, as if they have the right to decide for me what is right for my health, unless this bill was passed then the psychiatrists would be able to by-pass this process. Below is my testimony before the committee.

Testimony against HB 836

Court Ordered Treatment With Psychoactive Medication

March 30, 2011

Good Afternoon and thank you for allowing me this chance to speak to you today. My name is Evelyn Scogin and I am here today to testify against HB 836. I believe I am uniquely qualified to speak about the injury the passage of this bill will cause as I was injured by the same drugs and psychiatric system that proposes this bill. When I was most vulnerable and needed help to overcome the emotional problems I had, I turned to the current psychiatric system. I was coerced into taking drug after drug to solve my problems. Instead of helping, these same drugs made me so ill that not only did I have to stop working and go on disability, but I could no longer think or function as a rational human being. I was labeled and drugged into believing everything my psychiatrist told me. It wasn't until I was rushed to the hospital with a suspected heart attack that I discovered those same drugs were killing me. In fact I am now diabetic and had thyroid cancer due to two of the drugs I was taking and recently, two years after getting off all of the drugs, I have developed a head tremor. It is a proven fact that people who are on these types of drugs for any length of time die an average of 25 years earlier than normal.

Only after withdrawing from the drugs did I become a healthy functioning human being again. Only recently have I been able to return to part time work. If a bill such as this had been passed into law when I decided, against my psychiatrist's orders to stop taking these drugs, I would at the very least still be sitting in my room like a vegetable and perhaps have died due to the severe side effects of my so called treatment. At least I had the right to decide for myself what was the right course of treatment, just as any of you sitting here would choose to do for yourself.

The current psychiatric system has led the public to believe that we who have had emotional distress have an illness that can be managed with drugs and electroshock. The truth is there is no basis in science for what they and the pharmaceutical companies would have us believe. They also want you to think that they have a right to protect us from ourselves. If you had a loved one who was suicidal and/or was believed to be harmful to others you would want action to be taken. It is a natural human emotion to care for those around us and want to protect them from harm. Psychiatry would then have us believe they have the right in this instance, to without due process take away all of our human rights. It is very easy to believe that you or a loved one would never end up in a situation such as I experienced, but that is just not the case. Do not allow psychiatry to mislead you into believing, as I did, that they have any more right than any other doctor to control how we choose to treat our bodies. Protect this most basic of all human rights and do not pass this bill into law. Thank you.

Being that this was the first time I had spoken to this type of group before I was understandably anxious. When I walked up to the podium I took a deep breath, remembered that I had a whole group of friends who had my back, I looked at the committee chairwoman in the eye and began my speech. As I began speaking I became angry all over again that anyone could just take away another's due process rights in such a blatant manner. My speech reflected my righteous anger and when I had finished, I again looked the committee members in the eyes and then thanked them for their time and returned to my seat. If not for the fact that any display of reaction from the crowd is forbidden I really felt that many people wanted to clap. I however, had to calmly return to my seat and wait for everyone to finish speaking before leaving. I spoke and wrote to representatives several times during this legislative session and each time I felt more and more that I had found myself again. I realized at this point I have traveled back from the underworld like Inanna. Like Inanna I have transformed myself from the abused victim to a heroine. Like many individuals who have gone through such a transformative process have found that I am not the same person I was before. While this is a good thing it can be a shock to those who knew you as a different person. Now I have begun to write my story both past and present by living it and writing it with each step I take along my heroine's journey. It has now become my job as Maureen Murdock states in her book, *The Heroine's Journey* "It is the job of the heroine to enlighten the world by loving it--starting with herself (159)."(3) To that end I have dedicated myself to love myself as I am and speak openly with love in order to enlighten those who read my words and that my dream of a world that cares for all as they wish to be cared for themselves comes to pass.

Descent

End Notes

Cover Photo:

1. Cover photo taken by Ileana van Kuartel, 2011.

Dedication Page

1. Dr. Seuss, from *The Lorax*, Random House Digital, p70.

Chapter 1:

1. Laing, R. D. from *The Politics of Experience* quoted by Leonard Roy Frank in *Quotationary,* Random House 2010, p.504.

Chapter 2:

1. Campbell, Joseph, from *The Hero With a Thousand Faces* quoted in website www.goodreads.com, 2012

Chapter 3:

1. Breggin, Peter R. from "Disabling the Brain with Electroshock" in Maurice Dongier and Eric D. Winkower, eds. *Divergent Views in Psychiatry* quoted by Leonard Roy Frank in *Quotationary*, Random House 2010, p.677.

Chapter 4:

1. Frame, Janet from *Faces in the Water* quoted by Leonard Roy Frank in *Quotationary*, Random House 2010, p.786.

Chapter 5:

1. Szasz, Thomas from Introduction to *The Manufacture of Madness: A Comparative Study of the Inquisition and the Mental Health Movement* quoted by Leonard Roy Frank in *Quotationary*, Random House 2010, p.679.

Chapter 6:

1. Jong, Erica from "Alcestis on the Poetry Circuit" quoted by Maureen Murdock in *The Heroine's Journey*, Shambhala 1990, p.54

Chapter 7:

1. Lamott, Anne from Introduction to *Bird by Bird: Some Instructions on Writing and Life* quoted by Leonard Roy Frank in *Quotationary*, Random House 2010, p.371.

Chapter 8:

1. Arnot, Robert E. from "Observations on the Effects of Electric Convulsive Treatment in Man-Psychological," *Diseases of the Nervous System* quoted

by Leonard Roy Frank in *Quotationary*, Random House 2010, p.785

2.Silverman, Harold M. Pharm. D., *The Pill Book The New And Revised 14th Edition,* Bantam Books, 2010, pp. 62, 274, 372, 629, 656, 881, 931, 1113, 1121, 1192, 1227, 1231.

Chapter 9:

1. Campbell, Joseph, *The Hero With A Thousand Faces,* New World Library, 2008, p.337.

2. Szasz, Thomas, quoted by Lenoard Roy Frank edt., *The History of Shock Treatment*, Leonard Roy Frank, 1978.

Chapter 10:

1. Campbell, Joseph, The Hero With A Thousand Faces, New World Library, 2008, p.18.

2. Breeding, John and Scogin, Evelyn, *One Woman's Near Destruction and Reemergence from Psychiatric Assault: The Inspiring Story of Evelyn Scogin,* Journal of Humanistic Psychology, 2012, volume 52, number 1, pp. 53-72.

3. Murdock, Maureen, *The Heroine's Journey, Shambhala, 1910, p.159.*

Descent